A Frenchman born in 1958, **Marc HALTER** is a teacher who is passionate about history and philosophy. The History of the Maginot Line has been part of his life since his birth. His grandfather Nicolas worked for several years on the construction of Fort Hochwald, and his father Emile served as an officer in 1940 at the Fort of Galgenberg. Marc Halter is head of the Society of Combat Veterans of the Maginot Line of the Haguenau Sector, and President of the Association of the Friends of the Maginot Line and Fort Schoenenbourg, which he has presented to thousands of tourists from all over the world. Author of numerous articles and essays, he is committed to establishing an accurate history of the period and to the rehabilitation of the memory of the combat veterans.

Brian B. Chin, an American, born in 1950, has a degree in history from the University of California. He has worked in Hollywood for 20 years as an artist and writer in television animation, as well as in film special effects. For 5 years he created comic strips on the Internet. Because of his interest in military history of the 20th Century, he created scale models and dioramas, notably for a military museum in San Francisco. He is the author of a book on the harbor defenses of San Francisco as well as a graphic album on the taking of a German fort at Metz in 1944.

Since 2004, the **Moselle River 1944** Association has been dedicated to honoring the soldiers who liberated Lorraine and Alsace in the Fall of 1944, recognizing in particular the Third Army's crossing of the Moselle River. **Moselle River 1944** works for the development of historically related tourism and the maintainance of French military heritage.

The Maginot Line constitutes a monumental heritage of technical, architectural and military value that is worth rediscovering. The fortress is visited from the north to the south of France, along 700km of the French border, by visitors from all over the world.

This is in part a way to bring people together.

THE GREAT WAR. AT VERDUN, LIKE ALL THE WAR FRONTS, FROM 1914 TO 1918, THOUSANDS OF MEN FIGHT AND DIE IN HORRIBLE COMBAT.

HISTORY OF THE
MAGINOT LINE

AT VERDUN, DESPITE THE LOSS OF FORT DOUAUMONT, THE FORTS CONTINUE TO RESIST BOMBARDMENT AND ATTACKS. IN JUNE A BATTLE TAKES PLACE IN THE GAS-FILLED TUNNELS OF THE FORT DE VAUX.

I'M FINISHED! I'M DYING OF THIRST!

HOLD ON! WE HAVE TO FIGHT ON!

40% OF ALL FRENCH MEN ARE MOBILIZED FOR THE WAR EFFORT. THROUGHOUT ALL OF FRANCE, WOMEN REPLACE THE MEN IN THE FACTORIES AND FIELDS.

DURING THE 51 MONTHS THE FRENCH MEN ARE AT THE FRONT THE BIRTH RATE CONTINUES TO DROP. BY 1934 THE FRENCH ARMY WILL BE SHORT OF THOUSANDS OF MEN (THIS IS CALLED THE "EMPTY CLASS" OF RECRUITS).

HONEY, I DON'T KNOW WHEN I'LL BE BACK.

WE'LL WAIT UNTIL THE WAR'S OVER AND YOU COME BACK TO START A FAMILY.

IN 1917 THE UNITED STATES DECLARES WAR ON GERMANY. AMERICAN SOLDIERS ARRIVE TO REINFORCE THE ALLIES ALONG THE WESTERN FRONT.

FINALLY, AFTER SO MUCH SACRIFICE THE ARMISTICE IS SIGNED ON 11 NOVEMBER 1918.

I'VE FOUGHT SO MY SON WILL NEVER HAVE TO KNOW WAR.

THIS WILL BE THE LAST WAR. YOU'LL SEE...THIS IS THE WAR TO END ALL WARS.

2.

THE COST OF THE WAR FOR FRANCE IS TERRIBLE; 1.4 MILLION DEAD AND 3 MILLION WOUNDED. TOWNS AND ENTIRE REGIONS ARE DEVASTATED WITH BILLIONS IN DAMAGES. ALL MUST BE REBUILT.

FRENCH TROOPS ENTER STRASBOURG ON 22 NOVEMBER 1918. FRANCE RECLAIMS ALSACE AND MOSELLE WHICH HAD BEEN ANNEXED BY GERMANY AFTER THE WAR OF 1870.

IN ALSACE AND LORRAINE THE FRENCH TAKE CONTROL OF THE GERMAN FORTS (FESTEN) OF METZ, MUTZIG, STRASBOURG, AND THIONVILLE. ENGINEERS NOW HAVE THE OPPORTUNITY TO STUDY THEM IN DETAIL AND ARE INSPIRED BY THEIR TECHNICAL ASPECTS.

ON 28 JUNE 1919 A PEACE TREATY IS SIGNED AT VERSAILLES. GERMANY IS REQUIRED TO PAY MASSIVE WAR DAMAGES AND HER ARMY IS LIMITED TO 100,000 MEN. FOR GERMANY THESE CONDITIONS ARE DEVASTATING.

UNDER THE CONDITIONS OF THE TREATY OF VERSAILLES THE FRENCH ARMY WILL OCCUPY THE GERMAN RHINELAND ALL THE WAY TO THE SARRE RIVER. THEY ARE OBLIGATED TO EVACUATE BY 1935. IN 1919 THE UNITED STATES SENATE FAILS TO RATIFY THE TREATY.

IN 1920, THE SUPREME WAR COUNCIL (CSG), AFTER LONG DISCUSSIONS, DECIDE TO STUDY A STRATEGY TO PUT IN PLACE A PLAN TO DEFEND THE NORTHEAST FRONTIER OF FRANCE.

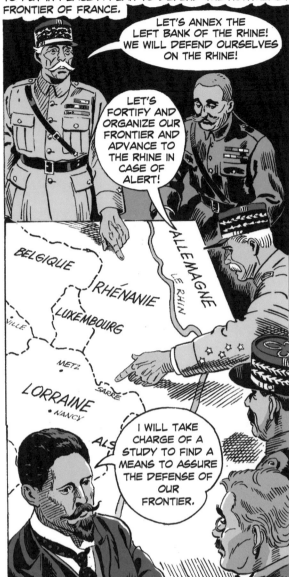

LET'S ANNEX THE LEFT BANK OF THE RHINE! WE WILL DEFEND OURSELVES ON THE RHINE!

LET'S FORTIFY AND ORGANIZE OUR FRONTIER AND ADVANCE TO THE RHINE IN CASE OF ALERT!

I WILL TAKE CHARGE OF A STUDY TO FIND A MEANS TO ASSURE THE DEFENSE OF OUR FRONTIER.

IN 1922 THE COMMISSION FOR THE DEFENSE OF THE TERRITORY (CDT) IS CREATED. THE COMMISSION PROPOSES THE DEVELOPMENT OF FORTIFIED REGIONS TO BLOCK THE 4 MAIN INVASION ROUTES: MOSELLE VALLEY, PLATEAU OF LORRAINE, RHINE PLAIN, AND THE BELFORT GAP.

WE MUST BLOCK THE INVASION ROUTES, LIKE THE MOSELLE VALLEY.

WE MUST PROTECT THE INDUSTRIAL BASIN OF LORRAINE.

WHAT ABOUT OUR BELGIAN AND SWISS BORDERS?

WE HAVE A DEFENSE TREATY WITH BELGIUM!

IN 1925 THE MINISTER OF DEFENSE, PAUL PAINLEVÉ, ESTABLISHES THE COMMISSION FOR THE DEFENSE OF THE FRONTIERS (CDF). THE CDF DEFINES THE BASIC OUTLINE, GENERAL STYLE, AND ORGANIZATION OF THE FORTIFICATIONS. THE CDF WILL PROVIDE A PRELIMINARY ESTIMATE OF COSTS.

THIS VALLEY IS QUITE VULNERABLE. IT HAS NO NATURAL DEFENSES.

THOSE TWO HILLS WOULD MAKE AN EXCELLENT LOCATION FOR CASEMATES!

IN APRIL 1927 THE MILITARY ENGINEER BUREAUS CHARGED WITH OVERSEEING THE CONSTRUCTION AND THE TECHNICAL INSPECTION OF THE FORTIFICATIONS (I.T.T.F.) WERE ESTABLISHED.

DIRECTION DES TRAVAUX DU GÉNIE

IN SEPTEMBER 1927 WAR MINISTER PAUL PAINLEVÉ ESTABLISHES THE COMMISSION FOR THE ORGANIZATION OF THE FORTIFIED REGIONS (CORF). THE CORF DEVELOPS THE OVERALL SCHEME FOR THE DEFENSES OF FRANCE, DRAWS UP THE PLANS FOR THE INDIVIDUAL FORTS, CONDUCT STUDIES FOR NEW ARMAMENTS, OBTAIN FUNDING, AND SOLICIT CONTRACTS FOR THE WORK TO BUILD THE FORTS.

IN ORDER TO HAVE A STRONG ARTILLERY FORT, WE MUST CONCENTRATE THE CANNONS.

FORT MASSE

FORT PALMÉ

I THINK THAT DISPERSING THE GUNS THROUGHOUT THE TERRAIN AND LINKING THE CASEMATES BY UNDERGROUND TUNNELS WILL BE MORE EFFECTIVE.

IN 1927, ITALY'S BENITO MUSSOLINI SEIZES ALL PROPERTIES BELONGING TO THE ITALIAN ROYAL FAMILY.

WE WILL RETAKE NICE, SAVOY, CORSICA, AND TUNISIA!

VIVA! NIZZA! SAVOIA!

THE CORF MAKES PLANS FOR TWO FORTIFIED REGIONS IN THE NORTHEAST: THE FORTIFIED REGION OF METZ (RFM), AND THE FORTIFIED REGION OF THE LAUTER [RIVER] (RFL). THE ALPS FACING ITALY WILL ALSO BE FORTIFIED AS WILL THE ISLAND OF CORSICA. IN TUNISIA FRANCE WILL CONSTRUCT THE MARETH LINE OF DEFENSES.

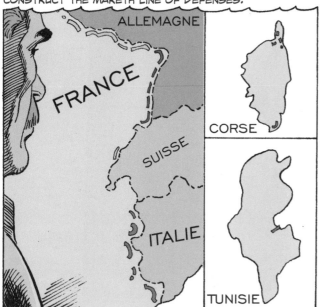

FRANCE IS NOW THREATENED BY GERMANY AND ITALY. SHE SIGNS A DEFENSE TREATY WITH BELGIUM, HOWEVER, SHE CANNOT COUNT ON ANY HELP FROM ENGLAND OR THE UNITED STATES. FRANCE MUST DEFEND AGAINST A SURPRISE ATTACK ON HER BORDERS AND AT THE SAME TIME BE ABLE TO MOBILIZE HER FORCES TO LAUNCH A COUNTERATTACK. THESE REQUIREMENTS CAN ONLY BE MET BY BUILDING A STRONG LINE OF FORTIFICATIONS.

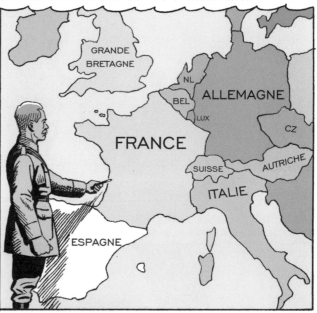

André Maginot

1877-1932 FRENCH POLITICIAN OF THE THIRD REPUBLIC. VOLUNTEERED TO SERVE IN THE ARMY IN 1914 AND SERVED AS A SERGEANT. SERIOUSLY WOUNDED AT VERDUN. MINISTER OF THE COLONIES AND PENSIONS AFTER THE WAR. BECAME MINISTER OF WAR IN 1929.

IN DECEMBER 1929 ANDRE MAGINOT PRESENTS LEGISLATION TO FUND THE FORTIFICATIONS PROJECT TO THE FRENCH PARLIAMENT. THE BILL IS VOTED ON AND ACCEPTED BY THE SENATE ON 14 JANUARY 1930, WITH A 90% VOTE IN FAVOR. THE BILL PROVIDES FOR A 5-YEAR CONSTRUCTION PROGRAM WITH A BUDGET OF 2.9 BILLION FRANCS (1.7 BILLION EUROS OR 2.35 BILLION DOLLARS).

CONCRETE IS MUCH STRONGER AND LESS COSTLY THAN A WALL OF BODIES.

YOUR PAPERS, PLEASE.

VLADIMIR KAROVSKI.

AFTER EXAMINING ALL CONTRACT BIDS ONLY FRENCH COMPANIES ARE CHOSEN TO BUILD THE FORTIFICATIONS. A PORTION OF THE WORKERS ARE FOREIGNERS. EACH WORKER'S BACKGROUND IS CAREFULLY CHECKED BY THE POLICE.

CHANTIER

ARTILLERY TESTS ON REINFORCED CONCRETE ARE CONDUCTED AT THE PROVING GROUND OF BOURGES. THE CORF ADOPTS 4 "DEGREES" OR LEVELS OF CONCRETE PROTECTION: PROTECTION 1 (1.5 METER THICKNESS) TO PROTECTION 4 (3.5 METERS). THE DENSITY OF THE CONCRETE COMPOUND IS 800KG OF CEMENT PER CUBIC METER.

THIS WALL RESISTS A CHARGE OF 300KG OF TNT.

NO SHELL OR BOMB WILL BE ABLE TO PIERCE IT.

IN 1930 WORK BEGINS ON THE FORTIFICATIONS. IN THE LARGE WORKS (*GROS OUVRAGES*), THE WORKERS BEGIN BY EXCAVATING SHAFTS FOR ACCESS FROM THE TUNNELS TO THE COMBAT BLOCS ON THE SURFACE.

6.

UNDERGROUND GALLERIES WERE CARVED OUT, CONNECTING TO SHAFTS THAT LED UP TO THE COMBAT BLOCS. PICKS AND JACK HAMMERS HELPED MAKE TUNNEL EXCAVATION EASIER. EXPLOSIVES WERE USED IN THE HARDER ROCK AND IN THE MOUNTAINS.

THE WORKMEN WERE PAID WELL BUT DUE TO TIGHT SCHEDULES GIVEN BY THE CORF THE WORK WAS DIFFICULT. ACCIDENTS FROM FALLS AND LANDSLIDES WERE FREQUENT.

THIS IS THE THIRD ACCIDENT THIS MONTH!

THEY MAKE US WORK SO QUICKLY!

HOW A CASEMATE IS CONSTRUCTED. AFTER EXCAVATION OF THE EARTH, WOODEN FORMS AND METAL REINFORCING RODS WERE ERECTED AND CONCRETE WAS POURED. AFTERWARDS THE METAL EMBRASURES AND ARMOR PLATING WAS ATTACHED TO THE CONCRETE. BY 1933, THE CORF EMPLOYED 25,000 WORKERS TO BUILD THE FORTIFICATIONS.

THE POURING OF THE CONCRETE NEVER STOPS.

WE ALWAYS HAVE AN ARMY ENGINEERING OFFICER PRESENT TO KEEP AN EYE ON THE WORK.

HOW A TURRET BLOC IS CONSTRUCTED. AFTER EXCAVATION OF THE EARTH, REINFORCING RODS AND ADVANCED ARMOR PLATING SURROUNDING THE TURRET IS PUT IN PLACE. THE HEIGHT OF THE BLOC COULD REACH 17 METERS. THE TURRET WAS INSTALLED LAST.

THE WORK SITES WERE IN OPERATION DAY AND NIGHT. BUILDING MATERIALS WERE BROUGHT TO THE SITES BY TRAIN, BY TRUCK, AND OCCASIONALLY IN SMALL CARTS. AT THE WORK SITES THE MATERIALS WERE MOVED IN SMALL WAGONS ALONG 60CM RAILWAYS.

THE WORKPLACE IS READY. CONCRETE IS PREPARED IN MOTORIZED MIXERS. THE VOLUME OF CEMENT IN CERTAIN BLOCS COULD BE AS MUCH AS 3000 CUBIC METERS. CONCRETE WAS POURED NON-STOP AND COULD CONTINUE FOR DOZENS OF HOURS.

ACCESS TO THE WORK SITES IN THE ALPS ALONG THE SOUTHEAST FRONTIER WAS DIFFICULT. MATERIAL WAS OFTEN TRANSPORTED TO THE SITE BY MULE OR BY CABLE CAR.

WE MUST TAKE ADVANTAGE OF THE WARMER WEATHER TO WORK UP HERE.

GUN TURRETS, OBSERVATION POSTS AND ARMOR PLATING WAS MANUFACTURED IN THE FACTORIES OF SCHNEIDER AT CREUSOT, BATIGNOLLES-CHÂTILLON AT NANTES, CHÂTILLON-COMMENTRY AT MONTLUÇON, THE FACTORIES OF THE LOIRE, AND OTHER SITES. IN 1932, THE COST OF THE ARMORED ELEMENTS WAS ESTIMATED AT 400 MILLION FRANCS (240 MILLION EUROS).

8.

GUN TURRETS AND OBSERVATION TOWERS (CLOCHES) COULD WEIGH AS MUCH AS 30 TONS. THEY WERE TRANSPORTED FROM THE FACTORIES BY TRAIN, THEN BY SPECIAL TRAILERS PULLED BY TRACTOR TO THE BLOCS AND CASEMATES FOR INSTALLATION.

WHEN THE CONCRETE WAS POURED AND HAD HARDENED AT BLOC OR CASEMATE, THE OBSERVATION POSTS AND DISASSEMBLED GUN TURRETS WERE DROPPED INTO THE SHAFTS USING A HEAVY DUTY GANTRY EQUIPPED WITH A WINCH.

ELECTRICITY WAS SUPPLIED TO THE FORTS THROUGH HIGH TENSION CABLES BURIED UNDERGROUND. CASEMATES AND OBSERVATORIES WERE INTERCONNECTED BY AN UNDERGROUND TELEPHONE NETWORK. JUNCTION BOXES PROTECTED BY CONCRETE, UNDERGROUND "JUNCTION CHAMBERS" CONNECTED THE FORTS TO EACH OTHER AND TO THE REAR COMMAND POSTS.

ONCE THE SHAFTS AND UNDERGROUND GALLERIES WERE COMPLETED, INSTALLATION OF THE INTERIOR ACCOMMODATIONS BEGAN. FORTS WITH ARTILLERY BLOCS WERE EQUIPPED WITH HEAVY DUTY ELEVATORS.

9.

A TEMPORARY 60CM RAILWAY NETWORK IS PLACED INSIDE THE GALLERIES DURING THE CONSTRUCTION PERIOD. IT IS USED TO REMOVE DEBRIS AND TO TRANSPORT MATERIALS TO BE USED IN THE FORT. WAGONS ARE PUSHED BY HAND ALONG THE RAILS.

ELECTRICITY IS SUPPLIED TO THE FORTS BY HIGH TENSION CABLES FROM THE OUTSIDE GRID. TRANSFORMER SUBSTATIONS CONVERT THE POWER TO LOW TENSION FOR USE THROUGHOUT THE CURRENT. ALTERNATING CURRENT IS CONVERTED BY THE TRANSFORMERS TO DIRECT CURRENT.

THE TRANSFORMERS PROVIDE A CONTINUOUS CURRENT FOR THE TRAINS AND THE GUN TURRETS.

POWER GENERATORS PROVIDE ELECTRICITY IN THE EVENT POWER FROM THE OUTSIDE GRID IS CUT OFF. TWO TO THREE GENERATORS ARE GROUPED TOGETHER TO PROVIDE BACKUP IN CASE OF BREAKDOWNS. THE MOTORS ARE POWERED BY DIESEL FUEL AND HAVE 2, 3, 4 OR 6 CYLINDERS.

SEVERAL FACTORIES FURNISH THE FORTS WITH GENERATORS: S.G.C.M., SULZER, C.L.M., S.M.I.M., ALSTHOM, BAUDOIN, AND RENAULT. A 200,000 LITER SUPPLY OF DIESEL WILL FUEL THE MOTORS FOR UP TO 3 MONTHS. WATER STORED IN LARGE TANKS WAS USED TO COOL THE ENGINES.

THIS TANK OF 100,000 LITERS CAN KEEP THE MOTORS RUNNING FOR 3 MONTHS.

DEFENSE DE FUMER

ELECTRICAL CABLES AND TELEPHONE LINES ARE PLACED INTO SLOTS IN THE GALLERY WALLS. THIS NOT ONLY PROTECTS THEM FROM DAMAGE (IF A SMALL WAGON DERAILS AND STRIKES THE WALL) BUT ALLOWS FOR EASY ACCESS FOR REPAIR.

THE CABLES ARE NOW IN PLACE. WE CAN EASILY REACH THEM IF THEY NEED TO BE REPAIRED.

PLACEMENT OF EQUIPMENT IN THE GREATER PART OF THE CASEMATES IS COMPLETED IN 1932 TO 1933. THEY ARE TYPICALLY EQUIPPED WITH A SMALL GENERATOR GROUP MANUFACTURED BY C.L.I.M. OR S.U.P.D.I. THEY ARE ALSO EQUIPPED WITH A SMALL WASH BASIN, A TOILET, ELECTRIC LIGHTS, AND VENTILATION.

MOST OF THE FORTS AND CASEMATES ARE LIT BY ELECTRIC LIGHT, HOWEVER, A SMALL NUMBER OF THE SMALLER BLOCKHOUSES USE PETROL LAMPS. LANTERNS WITH CANDLES ARE USED FOR EMERGENCY LIGHTING.

THE FORTS HAVE CHEMICAL TOILETS THAT DRAIN INTO A SEPTIC SYSTEM. WASTE FALLS INTO A RESERVOIR WHERE IT IS TREATED PRIOR TO BEING FLUSHED OUT WITH WATER.

IN PRINCIPAL, THE LARGE FORTS ARE EQUIPPED WITH A 60CM ELECTRIC RAILWAY. 16 ARTILLERY FORTS IN THE NORTHEAST HAVE A SMALL ELECTRIC TRAIN CALLED A "TROLLEY." THE LOCOMOTIVES OR "LOCO-TRACTORS" ARE MANUFACTURED BY VETRA OR S.W.

I HAVE HER UP TO 8KM AN HOUR!

THE SOLDIERS OF THE FIRST WORLD WAR WERE TRAUMATISED BY POISON GAS. THE FORTS AND CASEMATES ARE EQUIPPED WITH FILTERS TO BLOCK OUT POISON GAS. THE AIR INSIDE THE FORTS WAS PLACED IN A CONDITION OF NEGATIVE SUPPRESSION (AIR FLOWING OUT BUT NOT IN), TO KEEP THE GAS FROM GETTING INSIDE. FRESH AIR FROM THE OUTSIDE PASSED THROUGH THE FILTERS THEN INTO THE FORT.

THE MEN SLEPT IN CHAMBERS EQUIPPED WITH BUNK BEDS OR HAMMOCKS FIXED TO HOOKS IN THE WALL. THEY ALSO HAD AN INFIRMARY WITH AN OPERATING ROOM.

THE FORTS AND PERSONNEL SHELTERS WERE EQUIPPED WITH MODERN ELECTRIC, COAL, OR FUEL-POWERED KITCHENS. IN THE CASEMATES, FOOD WAS HEATED UP ON ELECTRIC PLATES. WATER CAME FROM UNDERGROUND WELLS WHERE IT WAS FILTERED AND STORED IN LARGE RESERVOIRS INSIDE THE FORTS.

EVERYTHING IS ELECTRIC HERE.

EVEN THE POTATO PEELER!

IN 1930 THE FRENCH ARMY ENDS THEIR OCCUPATION OF THE RHINELAND. ADOLF HITLER TAKES POWER IN GERMANY IN 1933. IN 1934 A NEW LAW IS ENACTED THAT BUDGETS 1275 MILLION MORE FRANCS (850 MILLION EUROS) TO BUILD A SMALL EXTENSION OF THE FORTRESS LINE.

12.

NUMEROUS BARRACKS AND MILITARY CAMPS ARE BUILT TO HOUSE THE FORTRESS TROOPS DURING PEACETIME. THE TROOPS RESIDE IN CLOSE PROXIMITY TO THEIR ASSIGNED FORTS. SPECIAL FIRING RANGES EQUIPPED WITH FORTRESS ARMAMENTS ARE BUILT FOR TRAINING.

STRATEGIC ROADS AND 60CM RAILWAY NETWORKS CONNECT THE FORTS WITH MUNITIONS AND SUPPLY DEPOTS TO THE REAR OF THE FORTIFIED POSITION. IN THE ALPS, ROAD BUILDING IS MORE DIFFICULT.

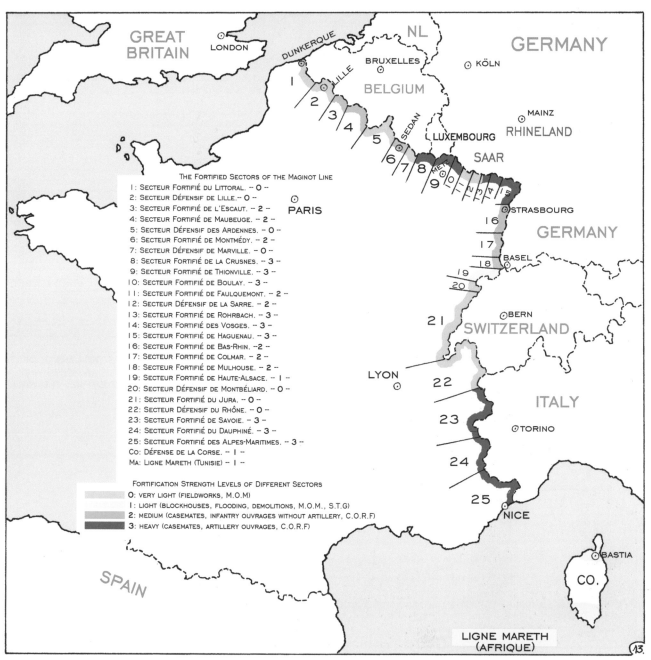

The Fortified Sectors of the Maginot Line

1: Secteur Fortifié du Littoral. -- O --
2: Secteur Défensif de Lille. -- O --
3: Secteur Fortifié de l'Escaut. -- 2 --
4: Secteur Fortifié de Maubeuge. -- 2 --
5: Secteur Défensif des Ardennes. -- O --
6: Secteur Fortifié de Montmédy. -- 2 --
7: Secteur Défensif de Marville. -- O --
8: Secteur Fortifié de la Crusnes. -- 3 --
9: Secteur Fortifié de Thionville. -- 3 --
10: Secteur Fortifié de Boulay. -- 3 --
11: Secteur Fortifié de Faulquemont. -- 2 --
12: Secteur Défensif de la Sarre. -- 2 --
13: Secteur Fortifié de Rohrbach. -- 3 --
14: Secteur Fortifié des Vosges. -- 3 --
15: Secteur Fortifié de Haguenau. -- 3 --
16: Secteur Fortifié de Bas-Rhin. -- 2 --
17: Secteur Fortifié de Colmar. -- 2 --
18: Secteur Fortifié de Mulhouse. -- 2 --
19: Secteur Fortifié de Haute-Alsace. -- 1 --
20: Secteur Défensif de Montbéliard. -- O --
21: Secteur Fortifié du Jura. -- O --
22: Secteur Défensif du Rhône. -- O --
23: Secteur Fortifié de Savoie. -- 3 --
24: Secteur Fortifié du Dauphiné. -- 3 --
25: Secteur Fortifié des Alpes-Maritimes. -- 3 --
Co: Défense de la Corse. -- 1 --
Ma: Ligne Mareth (Tunisie) -- 1 --

Fortification Strength Levels of Different Sectors

O: VERY LIGHT (FIELDWORKS, M.O.M)
1: LIGHT (BLOCKHOUSES, FLOODING, DEMOLITIONS, M.O.M., S.T.G)
2: MEDIUM (CASEMATES, INFANTRY OUVRAGES WITHOUT ARTILLERY, C.O.R.F)
3: HEAVY (CASEMATES, ARTILLERY OUVRAGES, C.O.R.F)

LIGNE MARETH (AFRIQUE)

TYPE	NAME OF FORT	FORTIFIED SECTOR	NUMBER OF BLOCS	NUMBER AND TYPE OF TURRETS	ARTILLERY IN CASEMATE
P.O	ETH	3	2	1 AM	
P.O	LES SARTS	4	2	1 AM	
P.O	BERSILLIES	4	2	1 AM	
P.O	LA SALMAGNE	4	2	1 AM	
P.O	BOUSSOIS	4	3	2 AM	
P.O	LA FERTE	6	2	1 AM	
G.O	LE CHESNOIS	6	6	1 AM 1 T75	
P.O	THONNELLE	6	4	1 AM	
G.O	VELOSNES	6	5	1 AM 1 T75	
P.O	FERME CHAPPY	8	2	1 MIT	
G.O	FERMONT	8	9	2 MIT 1 T81 1 T75	75 MM x 3
G.O	LATIREMONT	8	8	2 MIT 1 T81	75 MM x 6
P.O	MAUVAIS-BOIS	8	3	1 MIT	
P.O	BOIS-DU-FOUR	8	1	1 MIT	M 81 x 2
G.O	BREHAIN	8	10	2 MIT 1 T81 2 T75 1 T135	
P.O	AUMETZ	8	3	1 MIT	
G.O	ROCHONVILLERS	9	11	3 MIT 2 T75 2 T135	75 MM x 3 135 MM x 1
G.O	MOLVANGE	9	11	2 MIT 1 T81 3 T75 1 T135	
P.O	IMMERHOF	9	4	2 MIT 1 T81	
G.O	SOETRICH	9	8	2 MIT 2 T75 1 T135	M 81 x 2
P.O	BOIS-KARRE	9	1	1 MIT	
G.O	KOBENBUSCH	9	9	2 MIT 1 T81 1 T75	75 MM x 3
P.O	OBERHEIDE	9	1	1 MIT	
G.O	GALGENBERG	9	8	1 MIT 1 T81 1 T135	
P.O	SENTZICH	9	1	1 MIT	
G.O	METRICH	9	12	2 MIT 1 T81 2 T75 1 T135	M 81 x 2 75 MM x 3
G.O	BILLIG	9	8	1 MIT 1 T81 1 T75	75 MM x 4
G.O	HACKENBERG	10	19	3 MIT 2 T81 1 T75 2 T135	75 MM x 7 135 MM x 1
P.O	COUCOU	10	2	1 MIT	
G.O	MONT-DES-WELCHES	10	7	1 MIT 1 T81 2 T75	M 81 x 2
G.O	MICHELSBERG	10	6	1 MIT 1 T81 1 T75 1 T135	
P.O	HOBLING	10	4	1 MIT	
P.O	BOUSSE	10	4	1 MIT	
G.O	ANZELING	10	9	2 MIT 1 AM 1 T81 2 T75 1 T135	135 MM x 1
P.O	BERENBACH	10	3	1 MIT	
P.O	BOVENBERG	10	6	1 MIT	
P.O	DENTING	10	3	1 MIT	
P.O	VILLAGE DE COUME	10	3	1 MIT	
P.O	COUME NORD	10	1	1 MIT	
P.O	COUME	10	2	1 MIT	
P.O	COUME SUD	10	4		M 81 x 2
P.O	MOTTENBERG	10	3	1 MIT	
P.O	KERFENT	11	4	1 MIT	
P.O	BAMBESCH	11	3	1 MIT	
P.O	EINSELING	11	1	1 MIT	
P.O	LAUDREFANG	11	5	2 MIT	M 81 x 4
P.O	TETING	11	3	1 MIT	
P.O	HAUT POIRIER	12	4	1 AM	
P.O	WELSCHOFF	13	3	1 AM	
P.O	ROHRBACH	13	3	1 MIT 1 AM	
G.O	SIMSERHOF	13	10	2 MIT 2 T81 1 T75 1 T135	75 MM x 6 135 MM x 2
G.O	SCHIESSECK	13	11	1 MIT 1 T81 1 T75 1 T135	M 81 x 2
G.O	OTTERBIEL	13	5	1 MIT 1 T81	
G.O	GRAND HOHEKIRKEL	14	7	1 MIT 1 T75	
P.O	LEMBACH	14	3		
G.O	FOUR A CHAUX	14	8	1 MIT 1 T81 1 T75 1 T135	
G.O	HOCHWALD	15	14	2 MIT 1 T81 1 T75 2 T135	75 MM x 9 135 MM x 2
G.O	SCHOENENBOURG	15	8	1 MIT 1 T81 2 T75	

CHINA BUILT THE GREAT WALL ALONG THE LENGTH OF ITS FRONTIER. THE GREAT WALL KEPT OUT INVADERS WHO ATTEMPTED TO ATTACK THE CHINESE EMPIRE. THE WALL WAS FOR DEFENSIVE PURPOSES ONLY.

THE FRENCH FORTIFICATIONS WERE BUILT TO FULFILL A PRECISE MISSION. THEY MUST: DETER THE ENEMY FROM MAKING A SURPRISE ATTACK; COVER THE FRENCH TROOPS AS THEY MOBILIZE; ECONOMIZE FORCES TO MAKE UP FOR A SHORTAGE OF MANPOWER AS A RESULT OF LOSSES IN 1914 TO 1918; FORCE AN ATTACKER TO VIOLATE NEUTRAL TERRITORY (BELGIUM OR SWITZERLAND); AND TO SERVE AS A PLACE FROM WHICH TO LAUNCH A COUNTER OFFENSIVE.

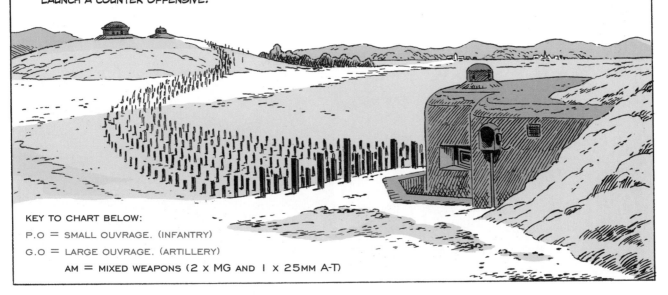

KEY TO CHART BELOW:

P.O = SMALL OUVRAGE. (INFANTRY)

G.O = LARGE OUVRAGE. (ARTILLERY)

AM = MIXED WEAPONS (2 x MG AND 1 x 25MM A-T)

OUVRAGES OF THE SOUTHEAST (ALPS)

TYPE	NAME OF FORT	FORTIFIED SECTOR	NUMBER OF BLOCS	NUMBER OF TURRETS	ARTILLERY IN CASEMATE
P.O	CHATELARD	23	1		
P.O	CAVE A CANON	23	1		
G.O	SAPEY	23	5		75 MM X 4
G.O	SAINT GOBAIN	23	5		M 81 X 4
G.O	SAINT ANTOINE	23	3		M 81 X 4 ; 75 MM X 2
G.O	LE LAVOIR	23	7		M 81 X 4 ; 75 MM X 6
G.O	PAS DU ROC	23	5		M 81 X 4 ; 75 MM X 2
P.O	ARRONDAZ	23	4		
P.O	LES ROCHILLES	23	4		
G.O	JANUS	24	8		M 81 X 2 ; 75 MM X 2 ; 95 MM X 4
P.O	COL DE BUFFERE	24	2		
P.O	COL DU GRANON	24	3		
P.O	LES AITTES	24	4		
P.O	GONDRAN	24	3		
G.O	ROCHE LACROIX	24	6	1 T75	M 81 X 2 ; 75 MM X 2
G.O	SAINT OURS HAUT	24	5		M 81 X 4 ; 75 MM X 1
P.O	PLATE LOMBARDE	24	4		
P.O	NORD OUEST DE FONTVIVE	24	2		
P.O	NORD EST DE ST OURS	24	2		
P.O	BAS DE ST OURS	24	1		
P.O	ANCIEN CAMP	24	2		
G.O	RESTEFOND	24	3		75 MM X 3
P.O	COL DE RESTEFOND	24	3		
P.O	GRANGES COMMUNES	24	1		
P.O	LA MOUTIERE	24	3		
P.O	COL DE CROUS	25	2		
G.O	RIMPLAS	25	7		M 81 X 2 ; 75 MM X 6
P.O	FRESSINEA	25	3		
P.O	VALDEBLORE	25	3		
P.O	LA SERENA	25	1		
P.O	COL DU CAIRE	25	2		
P.O	COL DU FORT	25	2		
G.O	GORDOLON	25	3		M 81 X 4 ; 75 MM X 2
G.O	FLAUT	25	5		M 81 X 4 ; 75 MM X 2
P.O	BAISSE DE SAINT VERAN	25	1		
P.O	PLAN CAVAL	25	3		
P.O	LA BEOLE	25	3		
P.O	COL D'AGNON	25	3		
P.O	LA DEA	25	3		
G.O	COL DE BROUIS	25	3		M 81 X 4
G.O	MONTE GROSSO	25	7	1 T75 ; 1 T135	M 81 X 4 ; 75 MM X 2
P.O	CHAMP DE TIR DE L'AGAISEN	25	3		
G.O	L'AGAISEN	25	4	1 T75	M 81 X 4 ; 75 MM X 2
G.O	SAINT ROCH	25	4		M 81 X 4 ; 75 MM X 1
G.O	LE BARBONNET	25	2		M 81 X 2 ; 75 MM X 2
G.O	CASTILLON	25	5		M 81 X 4 ; 75 MM X 2
P.O	COL DES BANQUETTES	25	3		
G.O	SAINTE AGNES	25	6		M 81 X 4 ; 75 MM X 4 ; 135MM X 2
P.O	COL DES GARDES	25	4		
G.O	MONT AGEL	25	8	2 T75	
G.O	ROQUEBRUNE	25	4		M 81 X 4 ; 75 MM X 4
P.O	CROUPE DU RESERVOIR	25	2		
G.O	CAP MARTIN	25	3		M 81 X 4 ; 75 MM X 4

ACCORDING TO THE TREATIES OF PARIS AND VIENNA OF 1815, THE ALLIES WHO FOUGHT AGAINST NAPOLEON 1ST REALIGNED THE FRENCH BORDER TO MAKE IT DIFFICULT FOR FRANCE TO ORGANIZE LINES OF DEFENSE. THE DEFENSE OF NORTHEAST FRANCE RELIED ON BELGIUM AS A BUFFER ZONE. IN 1920 THE FRANCO-BELGIAN MILITARY ACCORD WAS SIGNED.

ONE DAY THE GERMANS WILL POUR IN FROM THERE.

IN 1936 BELGIUM ONCE AGAIN DECLARES HER NEUTRALITY. FRANCE DECIDES, FOR ALL INTENTS AND PURPOSES, TO LEAVE THE BELGIAN BORDER WITHOUT MAJOR FORTIFICATIONS. IF GERMANY VIOLATES BELGIAN NEUTRALITY THEN ENGLAND WOULD ENTER THE WAR ON THE SIDE OF FRANCE AND THE FRENCH ARMY WOULD MARCH INTO BELGIUM TO DEFEND HER NORTHERN INDUSTRIAL REGION AND TO ORGANIZE DEFENSES BEYOND THE BORDER AND TO SEIZE THE RHINELAND AND RUHR INDUSTRIAL REGIONS.

AFTER 1933, FORTRESS TROOPS WERE ESTABLISHED. IN THE NORTHEAST THEY WERE DESIGNATED FORTRESS INFANTRY REGIMENTS. IN THE SOUTHEAST ALPINE FORTRESS BATTALIONS AND ALPINE FORTRESS DEMI-BRIGADES.

HERE THERE IS NOTHING BUT DISCIPLINE AND EXCERCISE.

IN THE FORTIFIED SECTIONS THE ARTILLERY WEAPONS IN THE LARGE FORTS AND INTERVALS WERE OPERATED BY POSITIONAL ARTILLERY REGIMENTS AND MOBILE ARTILLERY FORTRESS REGIMENTS. ARTILLERYMEN ALSO SERVED IN THE OBSERVATORIES.

WE STORE THOUSANDS OF SHELLS IN THE M1 AND M2 MAGAZINES.

THE ENGINEERING SPECIALISTS IN THE FORTS WERE DESIGNATED ENGINEERING REGIMENTS (RG-*GÉNIE*). FIREMEN AND MECHANICAL ENGINEERS OF THE 1ST AND 2ND AND 18TH RG WERE ASSIGNED TO THE NORTHEAST. THE 4TH AND 28TH RG WERE ASSIGNED TO THE SOUTHEAST. THE TELEPHONE EQUIPMENT WAS TYPE TM 32. RADIO MODELS USED WERE F50, F250, R TYPE F AND OTCF.

25% OF THE SOLDIERS OF THE MAGINOT LINE WERE FROM FRONTIER PROVINCES. RECRUITS CAME FROM OTHER REGIONS TO COMPLETE THE MANPOWER REQUIREMENTS.

FROM	FOR THE FORTIFIED SECTOR
NORTH & PARIS	ALSACE & LORRAINE
BURGUNDY & FRANCHE-COMTÉ	RHINE-ALSACE
LYON	SAVOIE AND DAUPHINÉ
PROVENCE	MARITIME ALPS

GARE DE L'EST

ALL ABOARD FOR ALSACE!

PLEASE HOLD, I WILL PUT YOU THROUGH TO EXTENSION 0.800.

THE CASEMATES AND FORTS BECOME ASSOCIATED AS "VESSELS OF WAR," COMPARABLE TO NAVAL VESSELS ON LAND, IN TERMS OF THE NUMBER OF SOLDIERS SERVING IN EACH AND THEIR DAILY ROUTINES. THEY EACH SERVE A ROTATIONAL TOUR OF DUTY: WATCH, GUARD, REST.

THREE DAYS IN THIS ROOM THEN 3 DAYS IN THE COMBAT BLOC.

AND WE'RE NOT PERMITTED TO LEAVE HERE.

BEGINNING IN 1935 THE PRESS BEGAN TO USE THE TERM "MAGINOT LINE" TO DESCRIBE THE FORTIFIED FRONTIER. THE WORD "LINE" WAS SELECTED AS A PROPAGANDA TERM USED TO CREATE THE IMPRESSION OF A CONTINUOUS DEFENSIVE LINE.

LA LIGNE MAGINOT PROTÈGE NOS FRONTIÈRES

AFTER A PLEBISCITE IN WHICH THE INHABITANTS CHOOSE TO JOIN WITH GERMANY, HITLER REOCCUPIES THE SARRE REGION IN 1935. HE BRINGS BACK OBLIGATORY SERVICE AND BEGINS TO REARM THE GERMAN ARMY, THE "WEHRMACHT," IN VIOLATION OF THE TREATY OF VERSAILLES.

IN 1935, GENERAL GAMELIN, THE NEW CHIEF OF STAFF OF THE FRENCH ARMY, DECIDES TO CONSTRUCT A CONTINUOUS LINE OF LIGHT FORTIFICATIONS. HE ALSO ORDERS THE CLOSING UP OF ANY GAPS LEFT BETWEEN THE LARGE WORKS BUILT BY THE CORF.

I'M PERFORMING MY MILITARY SERVICE BUT I'M DOING THE WORK OF A MASON!

AND WE NOW HAVE TO SERVE FOR TWO YEARS!

TO CONSTRUCT THE SMALL BLOCKHOUSES OF THE NEW LINE IN THE MOST ECONOMIC WAY POSSIBLE, THE ARMY USES SOLDIERS TO COMPLETE THE WORK. MORE THAN 5,000 SMALL BLOCS ARE BUILT USING THE "MILITARY HANDYWORK" (MAINS D'OEUVRE MILITAIRE--M.O.M.) OF SOLDIERS DURING THEIR TERMS OF OBLIGATORY SERVICE.

18.

STEEL RAILS USED BY THE RAILROADS WERE DRIVEN INTO THE EARTH TO CREATE AN ANTI-TANK OBSTACLE. THE WORKERS USED A PILE DRIVER AND BRUTE FORCE TO POUND THE RAILS INTO THE GROUND.

LET'S GO, GUYS, PULL!

THE CONSTRUCTION OF THE FORTIFICATIONS DID NOT KEEP THE FRENCH ARMY FROM ALSO DEVELOPING MOTORIZED UNITS, INCLUDING TANKS. IN 1940 THE FRENCH ARMY HAD MORE MECHANIZED TROOPS AND TANKS THAN THE WEHRMACHT.

BY 1935 THE FORTIFICATIONS WERE NEARLY OPERATIONAL...

Completed forts

	NORTH EAST	SOUTH EAST (ALPS)	TOTAL
ARTILLERY FORTS	23 (201 pieces)	23 (137 pieces)	46 (338 artillery pieces)
INFANTRY FORTS	36	61	97
CASEMATES	308	34	312
SHELTERS	80	0	80
OBSERVATORIES	14	3	17
SMALL BLOCKHOUSES (Built between 1935 & 1940)	3500	900	4400

AND:

-16 CASEMATES (4 WITH 75MM CANNONS) IN CORSICA
-61 BLOCKHOUSES ON THE MARETH LINE IN TUNISIA

ALL THE ROADS LEADING TO THE FRONTIER ARE GUARDED BY FORTIFIED HOUSES. IN CASE OF SURPRISE ATTACK THE GENDARMES WILL BLOCK THE ROAD WITH A "QUICK GATE," THAT WILL GIVE THEM TIME TO SET OFF EXPLOSIVES TO DESTROY THE ROAD AND SOUND THE ALERT.

IN CASE OF ATTACK WE WILL GIVE THE ALERT.

THE GENDARMES OF THE REPUBLICAN MOBILE GUARD (GRM) MAN THE FORTIFIED HOUSES. RESERVISTS FROM VILLAGES ALONG THE BORDER FORM FRONTIER GUARD UNITS. THEY PATROL ALONG THE BORDER.

EVERYTHING OK?

GOOD. NOTHING TO REPORT.

SMALL BLOCKHOUSES HAVE BEEN BUILT 2 TO 3 KILOMETERS FROM THE FRONTIER. THEY ARE ARMED WITH HOTCHKISS MACHINE GUNS, 25MM ANTI-TANK GUNS, OR WITH OLDER 47MM NAVAL CANNONS. THESE "ADVANCE POSTS" CONSTITUTE THE FIRST LINE OF RESISTANCE.

THE "PRINCIPAL LINE OF RESISTANCE" (LPR) IS SITUATED ABOUT 10KM FROM THE BORDER. THE LINE CONSISTS OF ANTI-TANK AND BARBED WIRE OBSTACLES, CASEMATES, AND COMBAT BLOCS OF THE INFANTRY AND ARTILLERY FORTS.

INFANTRY CASEMATES AND INDEPENDANT SMALL FORTS (PETITS OUVRAGES) CONSIST OF 1 OR 2 FIRING CHAMBERS, PROTECTED BY A DEEP DITCH AND ARMORED OBSERVATION POSTS. THEY PROVIDE FLANKING FIRE WITH ADJACENT CASEMATES TYPICALLY LOCATED 100 TO 1200 METERS AWAY.

THE "SIMPLE CASEMATE" HAS ONE FIRING CHAMBER AND A PLACE FOR THE TROOPS TO REST. THE CREW CONSISTS OF 12 SOLDIERS. THE "DOUBLE CASEMATE" HAS TWO FIRING CHAMBERS (LEFT AND RIGHT) AND TWO CREW REST CHAMBERS FOR 25 MEN. EACH FIRING CHAMBER HAS TWO EMBRASURES FOR THE 37 OR 47MM ANTI-TANK GUN PLUS TWIN MACHINE GUNS.

THE "CLOCHE (ARMORED CUPOLA) G.F.M." (WITH 3-FOLD MISSION OF OBSERVATION (GUETTEUR), RIFLE (FUSIL), AND MACHINE GUN (MITRAILLEUSE), SHELTERS THE OCCUPANT WITH 30CM THICK STEEL. IT HAS 3 TO 5 EMBRASURES FOR MULTIPLE PURPOSES AND COMES IN VARIOUS MODELS SUCH AS THE JUMELAGE MITRAILLEUSE (TWO 7.5MM MACHINE GUNS MAC 31), OR SOMETIMES THE TRIPLE CAPABILITY OF TWIN MACHINE GUNS PLUS A 25MM CANNON, (TRUMELAGE).

THE "CLOCHE V.D.P." (DIRECT OR PERISCOPIC VISION) IS FOR OBSERVATION. THE SUMMIT OF THE CUPOLA IS PIERCED WITH A HOLE FOR A PERISCOPE USED TO REGULATE FIRE. THE PERISCOPES ARE TYPE M, N, B, C, AND P2. 1550 CUPOLAS OF THIS TYPE WERE INSTALLED.

AFTER 1936 THE TECHNICAL ENGINEERING SECTION (SECTION TECHNIQUE DU GÉNIE - S.T.G.), PUT TOGETHER PLANS FOR CONSTRUCTION OF LIGHT CASEMATES AND BLOCKHOUSES TO REINFORCE THE "NEW FRONTS." THESE CASEMATES WOULD BE EQUIPPED WITH DISMOUNTABLE GUN TURRETS (MODEL 36) AND OTHER SCRAP METAL MATERIALS.

I HOPE THEY SEND US THE ARMORED EMBRASURES AND GUN PORTS IN TIME!

22

CONCRETE SHELTERS ARE BUILT TO THE REAR OF THE PRINCIPAL LINE OF RESISTANCE TO HOUSE THE INTERVAL AND FORTRESS TROOPS. TWO TYPES EXISTED: SURFACE SHELTERS AND CAVERN SHELTERS BUILT DEEP UNDERGROUND. SMALLER SHELTERS WERE BUILT IN THE ALPS AND ALONG THE RHINE.

THE 152 ECLIPSABLE TURRETS EACH MOUNT A GUN BATTERY AND CAN FIRE ALONG A 360 DEGREE AXIS. THEIR DIAMETER VARIES FROM 2 TO 4 METERS AND THEY WEIGH FROM 96 TO 265 TONS. THE STEEL ARMOR IS 30CM THICK.

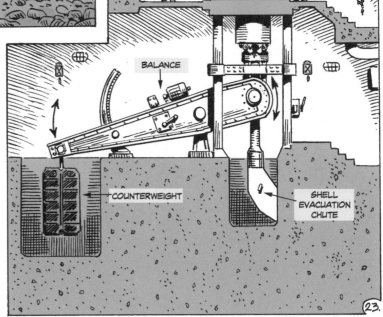

THERE WERE SEVERAL TYPES OF TURRETS...

TYPE of TURRET (T)	ARMAMENT
T 75 Model 32R	2 75mm short-barrel cannons
T 75 Model 33	2 75mm cannons
T Machine Gun	2 7.5mm machine guns
T 81 Model 32	2 81mm mortars
T 135 Model 32	2 135mm Bomb Throwers
T Mixed Arms	2 sets of 1 x Twin MG + 25mm AT

IN THE ARTILLERY FORTS, 75MM AND 135MM GUNS WERE PLACED IN POWERFUL CASEMATES. THE NUMBER OF GUNS VARIED FROM 1 TO 4. THESE ARTILLERY BLOCS PROVIDED FLANKING FIRE.

IN THE ALPS THERE WERE NOT MANY TURRETS. BECAUSE OF THE TERRAIN (RAVINES, DEFILES), MANY OF THE WEAPONS PROVIDED CURVING FIRE: 81MM MORTARS, 135MM BOMB THROWERS, AND THE 75MM MODEL 31. THE FORTS IN THE SOUTHEAST WERE MORE MASSIVE THAN IN THE NORTHEAST.

24.

MORTARS WERE USED FOR CURVING FIRE. THEY WERE PLACED IN PAIRS IN ECLIPSABLE TURRETS OR IN CASEMATES. IN THE LATTER CASE THEY WERE SITUATED AT THE BASE OF THE DITCH WHERE THEIR EMBRASURES WERE WELL PROTECTED.

THE RHINE DEFENSES WERE ASSURED BY 3 STAGGERED LINES OF CASEMATES:

1- THE CASEMATES ALONG THE BANK OF THE RHINE, AT THE POINTS OF PASSAGE

2- THE LINE OF SHELTERS IN THE FORESTS

3- THE LINE IN THE VILLAGES (THE PRINCIPAL LINE OF RESISTANCE)

THE MORTARS AT THE BOTTOM OF THE DITCH ARE INVISIBLE!

IN CASE OF FLOODING WE WILL PUT PANELS IN PLACE TO PROTECT THE EMBRASURES FROM RISING WATERS.

FLOOD ZONES WERE PREPARED IN CERTAIN AREAS: THE FRENCH SARRE AND NORTHERN ALSACE. RESERVOIRS AND DAMS WERE USED TO CONTROL THE WATER AND TO FLOOD CERTAIN AREAS TO PREVENT THE PASSAGE OF VEHICLES AND TANKS.

THE DEFENSE STRATEGY OF 1926 CALLED FOR THE MASSIVE DESTRUCTION OF FORESTS IN THE ARDENNES. THOUSANDS OF TREES WERE SCHEDULED TO BE CUT DOWN TO BLOCK STRATEGIC PASSAGES. THIS PROJECT WAS NOT CARRIED OUT BY 1940.

THE FORTS ARE IDENTIFIED IN 5 CLASSES. THEIR STRENGTH DEPENDS ON THE NUMBER OF COMBAT BLOCS INCLUDED IN THE ENSEMBLE; THE SMALL INFANTRY FORTS (PETITS OUVRAGES (WORKS)) WITH 1 OR MORE BLOCS, TO THE LARGE ARTILLERY FORTS (GROS OUVRAGES) WITH UP TO 19 BLOCS.

INFANTRY WEAPONS CONSIST OF 7.5MM TWIN REIBEL MACHINE GUNS, MODEL M.A.C. 31, MACHINE GUN RIFLES (F-M 24/29), 37 OR 47MM MODEL 34 ANTI-TANK CANNONS, SLOTS (GULLETS) TO LAUNCH HAND GRENADES INTO THE DITCH, AND SOMETIMES HOTCHKISS 13.2MM MODEL 30 MACHINE GUNS.

WE CAN REPLACE THE MACHINE GUNS WITH CANNONS IN THE SAME EMBRASURE.

THE FORTRESS ARTILLERY CONSISTED OF 75, 81, AND 135MM PIECES WITH A RANGE OF 300 TO 12,000 METERS. THE 75MM CANNON COULD FIRE AT A RATE OF 25 ROUNDS PER MINUTE.

YOU NEED TO BE SHORT AND THIN TO WORK IN HERE!

FOR THE RIGHT CANNON IT HELPS TO BE LEFT-HANDED!

26.

ARMAMENTS IN PLACE

WEAPON (caliber in mm)	EMBRASURE CASEMATE	CUPOLA	TURRET
Machine gun rifle 7.5mm Mod. 24/29	X		
Twin 7.5mm Mod. 31 machine guns	X	X	X
Machine gun 13.2mm Mod. 30	X		
Triple piece (7.5mm+25mm SA 34 cannon)	X	X	X
Mortar 50mm Mod. 35	X	X	X
Mortar 81mm Mod. 32	X		X
Howitzer 75mm Mod. 29, 31, 32, 34R, 33	X		
Howitzer 75mm Mod. 05R, 32R, 33	X		X
Bomb Launcher 135mm Mod. 32	X		X

THE ENTRANCES TO THE CASEMATES, OBSERVATORIES, AND SHELTERS WERE WELL PROTECTED AND DEFENDED BY EMBRASURES WITH THE MACHINE GUN RIFLE. TWO ARMORED DOORS WERE PLACED IN "CHICANE" (OFF-CENTER) AND A SMALL RETRACTABLE GANG PLANK PERMITTED PASSAGE ACROSS THE DITCH.

WE CAN RAISE THE GANG PLANK LIKE A DRAWBRIDGE IN A CASTLE!

THE SMALL FORTS POSSESSED A SINGLE ENTRANCE CALLED A "MEN'S ENTRANCE." THE LARGE FORTS HAD BOTH A MEN'S ENTRANCE AND A SECOND MUNITIONS ENTRANCE. SOME FORTS HAD A SINGLE, COMBINED ENTRANCE. CABLE CARS LEADING TO THE ENTRANCES WERE USED IN THE ALPS. RADIO ANTENNAS WERE INSTALLED ON THE FAÇADE OF THE ENTRANCE.

I NEED YOU TO DELIVER 40 TONS OF MUNITIONS FROM THE DEPOT.

DEPENDING ON THE SURROUNDING TERRAIN, ENTRANCES LED BACK TO THE INNER FORT'S UNDERGROUND GALLERIES VIA SHAFTS, STRAIGHT BACK INTO THE HILL, OR BY AN INCLINED PLAIN. ACCESS TO THE INNER FORT WAS PROTECTED BY AN ARMORED GRILL, A BRIDGE THAT COULD BE ROLLED OUT OF THE WAY TO REVEAL A DITCH, AND BY AN ENORMOUS ARMORED DOOR.

ABOVE ALL, DON'T FORGET! NO ONE IS ALLOWED TO USE THE ELEVATOR OR THE TRAIN.

IN MARCH 1936, HITLER REOCCUPIES THE GERMAN RHINELAND. THE FRENCH GOVERNMENT DOES NOT INTERVENE. BELGIUM DECLARES NEURALITY AND BREAKS ALL DEFENSE TREATIES WITH FRANCE. THE FORTRESS TROOPS ARE PLACED ON ALERT AND THE MAGINOT LINE BECOMES ACTIVE FOR THE FIRST TIME.

THE MINISTER OF WAR OR THE COMMANDER OF THE FORTIFIED REGION COULD TAKE THE PROPER MEASURES TO ACTIVATE THE FORTS OF THE MAGINOT LINE. THESE CONFIDENTIAL MEASURES PERMITTED THE FORTS TO BE PLACED IN A STATE OF DEFENSE WITHOUT TRIGGERING MOBILIZATION. LEVEL 10 ALERT; DELAY ONE HOUR. LEVEL 27 ALERT, REINFORCE; DELAY 18 HOURS, LEVEL 41...

DURING PEACETIME, THE SOLDIERS ARE LODGED IN BARRACKS, OR *CITÉS*, LOCATED OUTSIDE OF, AND TO THE REAR OF THE FORTS. IN CASE OF ALERT, THEY WOULD RAPIDLY OCCUPY THE FORTS, WITH EACH MAN HAVING A MISSION AND A PRECISE POST.

LEVEL 10! ALERT! THE FORTS MUST BE MANNED IN LESS THAN ONE HOUR!

HELLO, COMMAND POST, THIS IS OBSERVATORY 04! NOTHING TO REPORT IN SECTOR 12!

28.

IN PEACETIME, EACH FORTIFIED SECTOR IS DEFENDED BY A FORTRESS INFANTRY REGIMENT (OR D.B.A.F. IN THE ALPS); GENERALLY MADE UP OF 3 BATTALIONS. AFTER MOBILIZATION EACH BATTALION IS CONVERTED TO A REGIMENT TO DEFEND A SUB-SECTOR.

YOU HAVE THE MOST IMPORTANT MISSION: TO RESIST IN PLACE IN ORDER TO COVER MOBILIZATION.

THE FORTRESS CREWS ARE DIVIDED INTO COMPANIES OF CASEMATE TEAMS (C.E.C.), IN COMPANIES OF FORTRESS TEAMS (C.E.O.) AND TAKE THEIR POSITIONS IN THE CASEMATES OR THE FORTS AS WELL AS IN COMPANIES OF RIFLE PATROLS TO ASSURE THE DEFENSE OF THE INTERVALS BETWEEN THE FORTS.

OUR PATROL ZONE RUNS FROM CASEMATE 35/3 TO THE EDGE OF THE WOODS!

ONLY THE GUN TURRETS, THE CASEMATES, AND THE ENTRANCES ARE VISIBLE. THEY ARE CONNECTED BY GALLERIES AND CONSTITUTE THE BLOCS OF THE FORT. COMMUNICATIONS AND OTHER INFRASTRUCTURE IS UNDERGROUND, PROTECTED, AND INVISIBLE.

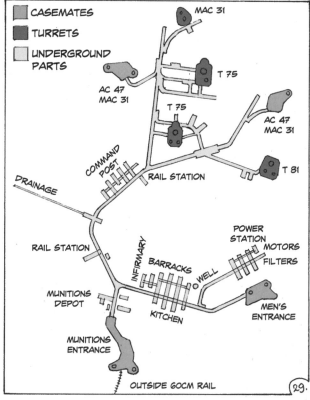

CASEMATES
TURRETS
UNDERGROUND PARTS

MAC 31

T 75

AC 47 MAC 31

T 75

AC 47 MAC 31

T 81

COMMAND POST

DRAINAGE

RAIL STATION

RAIL STATION

POWER STATION

MOTORS

FILTERS

INFIRMARY

BARRACKS

WELL

MUNITIONS DEPOT

KITCHEN

MEN'S ENTRANCE

MUNITIONS ENTRANCE

OUTSIDE 60CM RAIL

THE FORTS ARE PLACED IN A CONTINUAL STATE OF DEFENSE, NOTABLY FROM MARCH TO MAY 1938 DUE TO THE ANSCHLUSS (INCORPORATION OF AUSTRIA INTO THE GERMAN REICH), AND THEN IN SEPTEMBER BECAUSE OF THE SUDETEN CRISIS IN CZECHOSLOVAKIA.

AT THE END OF SEPTEMBER 1938 IT SEEMED THAT WAR WAS IMMINENT. MOBILIZATION IS ORDERED. ALL OF THE FORTS ARE ON ALERT. THE LAMENTABLE MUNICH ACCORDS PUT AN END TO THE TENSIONS. HITLER RECEIVES THE SUDETENLAND FROM CZECHOSLOVAKIA IN RETURN.

AFTER THE MUNICH ACCORDS, THE GERMANS OCCUPY THE CZECH FORTIFICATIONS. THE WEHRMACHT STUDIES THESE FORTIFICATIONS AND PROCEEDS TO CONDUCT TESTS TO DESTROY THEM. IN MARCH 1939 HITLER OCCUPIES THE REST OF CZECHOSLOVAKIA. THE CZECH ARMAMENT FACTORIES HELP TO EQUIP THE GERMAN DIVISIONS.

IT'S JUST LIKE THE FRENCH MAGINOT LINE!

AFTER THE SLAUGHTER OF THE GREAT WAR, MOST FRENCHMEN WOULD ACCEPT JUST ABOUT ANYTHING TO AVOID ANOTHER CONFLICT. THE POLITICIANS AND UNIONS ARE MOSTLY MADE UP OF PACIFISTS. THEY DECLARE WAR TO BE AGAINST THE LAW AND APPROVE OF THE "PHANTOM" PEACE.

BETTER TO LIVE AS A GERMAN THAN TO DIE A FRENCHMAN!

SLAVERY RATHER THAN WAR!

ON AUGUST 23RD 1939 THE NAZI FOREIGN MINISTER VON RIBBENTROP AND HIS SOVIET COUNTERPART, MOLOTOV NEGOTIATE A PACT. THEY SIGN, IN THE NAMES OF HITLER AND STALIN, THE GERMAN-RUSSIAN PACT. THE MAGINOT LINE IS ON ALERT BEGINNING AUGUST 21ST.

WELCOME TO THE SOVIET UNION HERR VON RIBBENTROP!

THE DANZIG CORRIDOR CRISIS IS A PRETEXT THAT ALLOWS HITLER TO ATTACK POLAND ON SEPTEMBER 1ST. ON SEPTEMBER 2ND FRANCE ORDERS GENERAL MOBILIZATION. ON SUNDAY, SEPTEMBER 3RD, GREAT BRITAIN AND FRANCE DECLARE WAR ON GERMANY.

ON SEPTEMBER 2ND, 1939, THE KLAXON SOUNDS AND THE VILLAGERS MUST EVACUATE THE ZONE IN FRONT OF THE FORTIFICATIONS. STRASBOURG AS WELL AS 550 COMMUNITIES IN ALSACE AND LORRAINE, CLOSE TO 600,000 PEOPLE, ARE EVACUATED. FROM THEIR CASEMATES, THE SOLDIERS WATCH THE DEPARTURE OF THEIR FAMILIES.

WHERE ARE WE GOING WITH OUR 30KG OF BAGGAGE, PAPA?

WHY MUST WE LEAVE OUR HOUSE OPEN?

ON SEPTEMBER 9TH THE FRENCH ARMY LAUNCHES AN OFFENSIVE IN THE SARRE REGION. TROOPS PENETRATE INTO GERMANY. IN ALSACE THE TURRET OF BLOC 7 BIS OF HOCHWALD OPENS FIRE TO COVER A BATTALION OF THE 3RD R.T.M. AT THE GERMAN FRONTIER.

BY THE END OF SEPTEMBER POLAND SURRENDERS. THE FRENCH SARRE OFFENSIVE COMES TO A HALT. GERMANS AND FRENCH KEEP WATCH ON EACH OTHER. FRENCH MINISTER OF PROPAGANDA GIRARDOUX, CALLS THIS "LA DRÔLE DE GUERRE," OR THE "ODD" WAR, ALSO CALLED THE "PHONY WAR."

FRENCH SOLDIERS, DON'T DIE FOR ENGLAND. MAKE PEACE WITH GERMANY!

WHY ARE YOU AT WAR?

IN ALL THE REGIMENTS AS WELL AS IN THE FORTS, BANDS OF SNIPERS ARE CREATED TO PATROL BETWEEN THE MAGINOT LINE AND THE GERMAN POSITIONS.

TO THE REAR OF THE MAIN LINE OF RESISTANCE, THE FRENCH INSTALL LARGE CALIBER RAILWAY GUNS. IF THE GERMANS BOMB METZ OR STRASBOURG, THE GUNS CAN STRIKE KARLSRUHE, LANDAU, OR SAARBRÜCKEN.

WE MUST PUT UP THE CAMOUFLAGE NETTING TO HIDE THE GUNS FROM THE GERMAN PLANES!

THE MAGINOT LINE IS USED AS A MIRROR OF THE FRENCH ARMY. THE DUKE OF WINDSOR, WINSTON CHURCHILL, MISS FRANCE, POLITICIANS, WRITERS, JOURNALISTS, AND NUMEROUS OTHER PERSONALITIES VISIT THE FORTS. OFTEN THEY ARE ALLOWED TO FIRE THE CANNONS.

DURING THE PHONY WAR, FILM NIGHTS OR THEATER SHOWS WERE ORGANIZED. ACTORS AND CABARET ENTERTAINERS CREATED A DIVERSION FOR THESE MODERN "TROGOLODYTES."

I WONDER WHAT MY WIFE IS DOING RIGHT NOW!

I'M SURE MY KIDS HAVE CHANGED!

THE LACK OF SUNLIGHT, PERMANENT ARTIFICIAL LIGHT, THE CRAMPED QUARTERS, AND LOUD NOISES WERE THE CAUSE OF A FORM OF DEPRESSION OF MORALE CALLED "BETONITE" (CONCRETITIS). OFFICERS AND NON-COMMISSIONED OFFICERS IMPOSED VERY STRICT DISCIPLINE.

IT SEEMS THAT, AT CHRISTMAS SOME OF US MAY GET LEAVE.

THAT'S POSSIBLE, BUT NOT FOR MORE THAN 10% OF THE GARRISON.

IN PRINCIPLE, THE FOOD RESERVES WOULD LAST FOR 30 DAYS. THE SOLDIERS EAT AT RETRACTABLE TABLES, OFFICERS' MEALS WERE SERVED IN A SPECIAL LOCATION.

MENU OF OCTOBER 25 1939
NOON: Beef Mironton and vegetables
EVENING: Tuna with beans

HERE IS THE SOUP FOR BLOC 2!

THAT SMELLS PRETTY GOOD!

HUNDREDS OF COLOR MURALS AND SKETCHES WERE PAINTED ON THE WALLS TO LIVEN UP THE CONCRETE WALLS OF THE FORTS. CERTAIN WORKS OF ART WERE DONE BY TRUE ARTISTS. PAINTINGS INCLUDED MOVIE STARS, CARTOONS, OR MILITARY SCENES.

I WILL PAINT THE SAME DESIGN IN THE STAIRCASE OF MY HOUSE!

THE WINTER OF 1939 TO 1940 WAS THE COLDEST OF THE CENTURY. EVERYTHING WAS PARALYZED. IN THE FORTS THE SOLDIERS CELEBRATED CHRISTMAS AND NEW YEAR. ECUMENICAL RELIGIOUS SERVICES WERE PROVIDED FOR THE TROOPS.

THE TROOPS ARE DIVIDED INTO FOUR GROUPS TO MAINTAIN FIGHTING EFFICIENCY: WATCH, SENTRY DUTY, AND REINFORCEMENT SERVICE IN THE COMBAT BLOCS. THEY ALTERNATE SHIFTS EVERY 8 HOURS. THE FOURTH GROUP IS RESTING IN THE BARRACKS OF THE FORT.

SILENCE IN THE RANKS!

DAY AND NIGHT THE SOLDIERS TRAIN TO HONE THEIR FIGHTING SKILLS. OBSERVATION AND FIRING MAPS ARE PLACED ON BOARDS AND PLOTTING TABLES. THESE ARE USED BY OBSERVERS, TELEPHONE SWITCHBOARD OPERATORS, TARGET PLOTTERS, AND ARTILLERY PLOTTERS TO COMMUNICATE RAPID (LESS THAN 1 MINUTE) AND PRECISE FIRING INSTRUCTIONS TO THE ARTILLERY COMBAT BLOCS.

OBSERVER 4 REPORTS OBJECTIVE 02, BEARING 135, DISTANCE 4250!

TRANSMIT THE COORDINATES OF OBJECTIVE 02 TO BLOC 4.

TO ALLOW THE MEN TO GET FRESH AIR THEY WERE PUT TO WORK OUTSIDE DIGGING TRENCHES AND ANTI-TANK DITCHES, AND RIGGING BARBED WIRE. OBSERVERS ALSO SCOPED OUT THE SURROUNDING TERRAIN TO IMPROVE THE TOPOGRAPHIC MAPS. THE MEN LIVED IN CONSTANT EXPECTATION OF APPROACHING COMBAT. THE REALITY OF THAT WOULD BE BRUTAL.

IN CASE OF ATTACK WE MUST BLOCK PASSAGE THROUGH THE VALLEY WITH AN ARTILLERY BARRAGE.

THE GERMAN ATTACK BEGAN IN THE WEST ON 10 MAY 1940. AT 0430 HOURS GERMAN GLIDERS AND PARATROOPS LANDED ON TOP OF BELGIUM'S POWERFUL FORT EBEN-EMAEL AND THE DEFENSES OF THE ALBERT CANAL. IN A FEW HOURS THE FORT IS NEUTRALIZED AND THE CANAL BRIDGES ARE CAPTURED. HOLLAND AND LUXEMBOURG ARE ATTACKED BY THE WEHRMACHT.

ON FRIDAY, 10 MAY 1940, AT 0630, THE KING OF BELGIUM CALLED THE ALLIES FOR HELP. IN THE AFTERNOON THE FIRST BRITISH AND FRENCH TROOPS ENTER BELGIUM AND LUXEMBOURG. THEY EXECUTE THE "DYLE" MANEUVER. BY EVENING, MOTORIZED FRENCH UNITS REACH THE NETHERLANDS.

ON 10 MAY THE 75MM TURRETS OF FORT DE BRÉHAIN FIRE 3800 ROUNDS IN SUPPORT OF THE FRENCH CAVALRY'S PENETRATION OF LUXEMBOURG. IN THE ARDENNES, IN A VERY LOPSIDED BATTLE, THE SMALL FORTIFIED HOUSES ALONG THE BORDER ATTEMPT TO BLOCK THE GERMAN TANKS.

THIS CRATER WILL SLOW DOWN OUR PROGRESS. CALL UP THE ENGINEERS TO FILL IT IN.

FROM THE 10TH OF MAY THE FORTS OF FERMONT, GALGENBERG, MÉTRICH, MOLVANGE AND ROCHONVILLERS HARASS THE WEHRMACHT CONVOYS COMING OUT OF LUXEMBOURG. BEGINNING ON 12 MAY FORTS FOUR À CHAUX, HOCHWALD, SCHOENENBOURG, AND SIMSERHOF POUND THE GERMANS ATTACKING THE ADVANCE POSTS IN ALSACE.

ON MAY 13TH, BETWEEN DINANT AND SEDAN, ALONG A 70KM FRONT, 45 WEHRMACHT DIVISIONS, INCLUDING 7 ARMORED DIVISIONS, ATTACK 6 BADLY EQUIPPED FRENCH RESERVE DIVISIONS. THE LUFTWAFFE CONTINUOUSLY BOMBS THE SMALL FRENCH BLOCKHOUSES IN THE SEDAN SECTOR. IN THE EVENING THE TANKS CROSS THE MEUSE AND STRIKE OUT TOWARDS THE WEST.

SCHNELL, WEG VON HIER!

FIRE DIRECTLY ON THE BLOCKHOUSE EMBRASURES. FIRE!

34.

FROM 1926, THE ARMY PLANNED FOR A MASSIVE PROGRAM OF DEMOLITIONS IN THE ARDENNES FOREST, YET, IN 1940 THEY HAD NOT BEEN COMPLETED. IN MAY 1938, FRENCH GENERAL PRÉTELAT COMMANDED A MILITARY EXCERCISE THAT ANTICIPATED A GERMAN ADVANCE THROUGH THE ARDENNES, SOMETHING THAT HAD NOT BEEN TAKEN SERIOUSLY INTO ACCOUNT. IN SEPTEMBER 1938 THE 7TH ARMY OF GENERAL GIRAUD IS IN RESERVE IN THE REGION OF REIMS, FACING THE ARDENNES. THE 7TH IS MOVED FURTHER TO THE NORTH IN NOVEMBER.

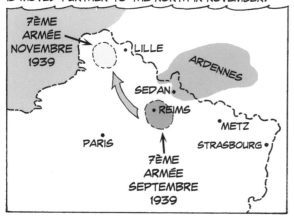

ON 10 AND 11 MAY THE 75MM TURRETS OF FORT VÉLOSNES AND CHESNOIS OPEN FIRE ON THE GERMANS CROSSING THE BELGIAN FRONTIER BEFORE MONTMÉDY. ON 16 MAY THE GERMANS ATTACK THE FORTIFIED VILLAGE OF VILLY WHICH WILL NOT BE CAPTURED UNTIL 18 MAY AFTER FEROCIOUS COMBAT.

ON 17 MAY THE GERMANS BOMBARD THE SMALL FORT OF LA FERTÉ. 88MM CANNONS DESTROY THE CUPOLAS. ON 18 MAY THE ENGINEERS LAUNCH AN ASSAULT ON LA FERTÉ'S 2 BLOCS. THEY NEUTRALIZE THE CUPOLAS AND THE MIXED ARMS TURRET WITH EXPLOSIVES (SHAPED CHARGES).

AFTER ANOTHER POUNDING AND A NEW ASSAULT, EXPLOSIONS CAUSE FIRES INSIDE BLOC 2 OF LA FERTÉ. THE 75MM TURRET OF CHESNOIS TRIED DESPERATELY TO CLEAR THE SURFACE. A FRENCH COUNTERATTACK USING TANKS IS LAUNCHED ON 18 MAY BUT THE FORT IS LOST.

THE SMALL FORT OF LA FERTÉ, THE LAST FORT OF THE MAGINOT LINE TO THE EAST OF SEDAN, SUCCUMBS TO THE ATTACK. LIKE AN ABANDONED WRECK AT THE BOTTOM OF THE OCEAN, SACRIFICING ALL OF THE MEN. ON THE NIGHT OF 18 TO 19 MAY 1940, THE GARRISON OF 105 SLOWLY DIE OF ASPHYXIATION.

MOVING WEST, THE GERMAN PANZERS ATTACK THE FORTIFIED SECTION OF MAUBEUGE BEGINNING ON 16 MAY. FROM 18 MAY THE SMALL FORTS OF BOUSSOIS AND SALMAGNE UNDERGO NUMEROUS ATTACKS FROM STUKA DIVE BOMBERS. FINALLY, ALL OF THEIR WEAPONS ARE DESTROYED AND THEY CEASE COMBAT ON 22 MAY.

FROM 22 MAY THE LAST 3 FORTS IN THE NORTH ARE SURROUNDED AND ATTACKED FROM THE REAR. FORT BERSILLIES CAPITULATES ON 22 MAY, LES SARTS THE 23RD, AND ETH ON THE 26TH. ON 20 MAY THE GERMANS HAVE REACHED THE SEA AND THE ALLIED ARMIES ARE CUT IN TWO.

DIRECT HIT ON THE EMBRASURE. JUST AS WE PRACTICED ON THE CZECH FORTS!

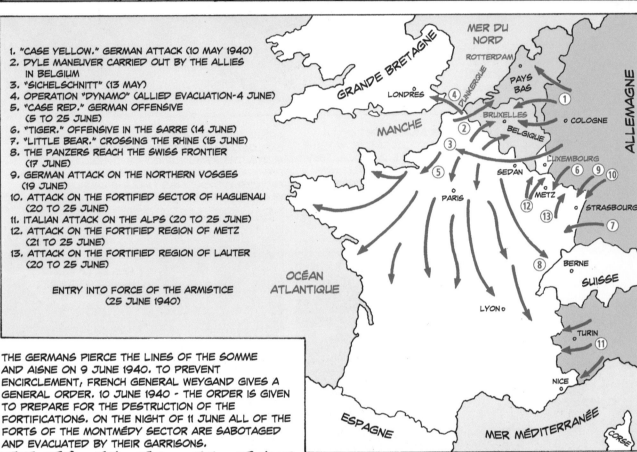

1. "CASE YELLOW." GERMAN ATTACK (10 MAY 1940)
2. DYLE MANEUVER CARRIED OUT BY THE ALLIES IN BELGIUM
3. "SICHELSCHNITT" (13 MAY)
4. OPERATION "DYNAMO" (ALLIED EVACUATION-4 JUNE)
5. "CASE RED." GERMAN OFFENSIVE (5 TO 25 JUNE)
6. "TIGER." OFFENSIVE IN THE SARRE (14 JUNE)
7. "LITTLE BEAR." CROSSING THE RHINE (15 JUNE)
8. THE PANZERS REACH THE SWISS FRONTIER (17 JUNE)
9. GERMAN ATTACK ON THE NORTHERN VOSGES (19 JUNE)
10. ATTACK ON THE FORTIFIED SECTOR OF HAGUENAU (20 TO 25 JUNE)
11. ITALIAN ATTACK ON THE ALPS (20 TO 25 JUNE)
12. ATTACK ON THE FORTIFIED REGION OF METZ (21 TO 25 JUNE)
13. ATTACK ON THE FORTIFIED REGION OF LAUTER (20 TO 25 JUNE)

ENTRY INTO FORCE OF THE ARMISTICE (25 JUNE 1940)

THE GERMANS PIERCE THE LINES OF THE SOMME AND AISNE ON 9 JUNE 1940. TO PREVENT ENCIRCLEMENT, FRENCH GENERAL WEYGAND GIVES A GENERAL ORDER. 10 JUNE 1940 - THE ORDER IS GIVEN TO PREPARE FOR THE DESTRUCTION OF THE FORTIFICATIONS. ON THE NIGHT OF 11 JUNE ALL OF THE FORTS OF THE MONTMÉDY SECTOR ARE SABOTAGED AND EVACUATED BY THEIR GARRISONS.

DRAIN THE OIL IN THE MOTORS AND LET THEM RUN UNTIL THEY BREAK DOWN.

I'VE TAKEN CARE OF THIS PERISCOPE FOR MONTHS AND NOW I'M BUSTING IT UP WITH A HAMMER!

STARTING ON 14 JUNE THE INTERVAL TROOPS BEGIN A RETREAT TO THE SOUTH. THE FRENCH GENERAL STAFF WANT TO HOLD OUT ON THE RHINE-MARNE CANAL AND ESTABLISH A LINE OF DEFENSE ON THE DOUBS AND LOIRE RIVERS.

CARRY ALL YOU CAN AND DESTROY THE REST!

HEAD SOUTH AND KEEP ABSOLUTE SILENCE!

ON 14 JUNE THE GERMAN FIRST ARMY LAUNCHED OPERATION TIGER, AN ATTACK ON THE SARRE GAP. THIS SECTOR OF THE MAGINOT LINE CONSISTS OF FLOOD ZONES AND SMALL M.O.M. BLOCKHOUSES. 1000 GERMAN GUNS AND THE LUFTWAFFE ARE ENGAGED. AFTER VERY DIFFICULT COMBAT FRENCH GENERAL HUBERT HALTS THE ADVANCE AND REPORTS VICTORY. MORE THAN 1000 GERMANS ARE KILLED. UNFORTUNATELY, ON THE EVENING OF 14 JUNE THE ORDER TO RETREAT IS GIVEN AND THE FRENCH PULL BACK.

IN ALSACE AND LORRAINE THE COMMANDERS OF THE FORTIFIED SECTORS DECIDE NOT TO LEAVE THEIR FORTS. THERE ARE MORE THAN 22,000 MEN WHO CONTINUE TO RESIST BEHIND THE CONCRETE AT THE SAME MOMENT THE WEHRMACHT MARCHES INTO PARIS.

THE RHINE CASEMATES ARE CUT OFF DUE TO THE WITHDRAWAL OF THE INTERVAL TROOPS TOWARDS THE VOSGES. ON 15 JUNE THE GERMAN 7TH ARMY CROSSES THE RHINE IN FORCE, LAUNCHING OPERATION SMALL BEAR. THE 88MM FLAK CANNONS DESTROY THE CASEMATES, AND "STORM BOATS" ARE SENT ACROSS THE RIVER. DESPITE THE DELUGE OF FIRE, THE FRENCH MANAGE TO HOLD OUT UNTIL THE END.

Among the first French Resistants

It is here, at the Command Post of Fort Schoenenbourg, on 14 June 1940, that the Commandant of the Fortified Sector of Haguenau, Lieutenant-Colonel Schwartz and other fortress commanders joined together and made the decision not to follow the orders to retreat and sabotage given by the High Command. They unanimously choose to remain loyal to the mission that was confided to them and for which they prepared and sacrificed. Loyal to their motto: "They shall not pass," they decided to resist in place. Thanks to their bravery, the fortress remained in French hands, unvanquished, after the Armistice of 25 June.

Plaque inaugurated by the Combat Veterans of the Maginot Line in August 2007

FROM THIS DISTANCE THE FRENCH BUNKERS DON'T STAND A CHANCE!

IN SOUTHERN ALSACE THE GERMANS TAKE 3 DAYS TO BREAK THROUGH 3 LINES OF CASEMATES. AT MARCKOLSHEIM, ON THE LINE OF FRONTIER VILLAGES, CASEMATES 34/3 AND 35/3 ARE ATTACKED BY STUKA DIVE BOMBERS, 88MM ANTI-AIRCRAFT GUNS, AND GERMAN ENGINEERS. NEARLY ALL OF THE MEN OF CASEMATE 34/3 ARE KILLED, BURNED BY THE GERMAN FLAME THROWERS.

THE FORTRESS TROOPS HAVE BEEN FIGHTING A REARGUARD ACTION SINCE 13 JUNE. ON 18 JUNE THEY ENGAGE IN BATTLE ALONG THE MARNE-RHINE CANAL AND CONTINUE TO RESIST IN THE VOSGES. THERE ARE ALREADY THOUSANDS OF CASUALTIES. TROOPS FIGHTING ON THE SUMMIT OF THE VOSGES MOUNTAINS SURRENDER BETWEEN 21 AND 28 JUNE.

OUT, OUT. COME ON OUT!

FOR 10 DAYS WE HAVE BEEN FIGHTING IN RETREAT.

I'M DONE. WE MARCH ALL NIGHT AND FIGHT ALL DAY.

WE'RE SCREWED. WE'RE COMPLETELY SURROUNDED. ALL OF THIS FOR THE SAKE OF HONOR.

ON 10 JUNE MUSSOLINI DECLARES WAR ON FRANCE. THE FRENCH ALPINE TROOPS BLOCK THE PASSES ALONG THE FRONTIER. ON THE SNOW-CAPPED SUMMITS THE EXCELLENT SKI PATROLS (S.E.S.) OBSERVE AND HARASS THE ITALIANS CLOSE TO THE BORDER.

THIS DECLARATION OF WAR IS A REAL STAB IN THE BACK!

ON 14 JUNE THE ITALIANS LAUNCH THEIR OFFENSIVE. 85,000 FRENCH SOLDIERS FACED 650,000 SOLDIERS OF *IL DUCE*, WHO BEGIN TO CROSS THE ALPINE PASSES. FRENCH ARTILLERY EFFECTIVELY COVERS THE ATTACK ON THE LINE OF ADVANCE POSTS WHICH RESIST FIERCELY.

THE ITALIANS MUST NOT GET THROUGH THE PASS!

ON 15 JUNE FORT MONTE GROSSO OPENS FIRE. HER CANNONS DESTROY MANY ITALIAN ARTILLERY BATTERIES. THE FORTS OF COL DE BROUIS, AGAISEN, AND BARBONNET PARTICIPATE IN A BARRAGE OF FIRE TO BLOCK THE ITALIAN TROOPS ATTEMPTING TO CROSS THE AUTHION MASSIF.

AIUTO, AIUTO!

VIENI QUI! AHG!

ON 21 JUNE THE ITALIAN FORT OF CHABERTON COMMENCES FIRE ON THE TOWN OF BRIANÇON IN THE HIGH ALPS. FOUR FRENCH 280MM MORTARS OF THE 154TH ARTILLERY REGIMENT OPEN FIRE. FORT JANUS KEEPS WATCH AND ENCOURAGES THE ARTILLERYMEN. AFTER JUST 57 SHOTS FORT CHABERTON IS REDUCED TO SILENCE.

OUR SECRET HAS BEEN WELL KEPT, LIEUTENANT!

YES, THAT MAKES 19 MONTHS OUR MORTARS HAVE BEEN IN PLACE!

JUST ON THE EDGE OF THE MEDITERRANEAN SEA, FORT CAP MARTIN COMES UNDER BOMBARDMENT. ON 23 JUNE THE ITALIAN INFANTRY LAUNCH A FRONTAL ATTACK. CAP MARTIN, COVERED BY FORTS ROQUEBRUNNE AND SAINTE AGNES, UNLEASH A VERITABLE HELLFIRE. FROM MENTON TO SOSPEL THE ITALIANS ARE STOPPED.

FROM MONT BLANC TO MENTON THE ARMY OF THE ALPS, COMMANDED BY GENERAL OLRY BLOCKS THE ARMY OF MUSSOLINI. THE CREWS OF FORTS ROCHE-LA-CROIX, SAINT GOBAIN, LAVOIR, AND ALL THE OTHERS RESIST AND CONTINUE TO POUND THE ITALIANS WITH FORMIDABLE EFFICIENCY. THE MAGINOT LINE IN THE ALPS FULFILLS ITS MISSION TO PERFECTION.

DISTANCE 5450 METERS, 16 DEGREES TO THE LEFT!

22 JUNE: THE ITALIAN ARMY ATTACKS THE MENTON REGION. THE FRENCH FORTS ARE BOMBARDED BY AIRCRAFT AND HEAVY ARTILLERY. THE 2 TURRETS OF FORT MONT AGEL DESTROY AN ITALIAN ARMORED TRAIN AS IT EXITS THE TUNNEL OF GARAVAN.

PRESTO, PRESTO! INTO THE TUNNEL!

100 METERS FROM THE ITALIAN BORDER, THE SMALL CASEMATE OF PONT SAINT-LOUIS RESISTS ALL ATTACKS. THE ITALIANS MUST GET BY THIS ADVANCE POST IN ORDER TO REACH MENTON. THEY ARE STOPPED AT THE PRINCIPAL LINE OF RESISTANCE BY THE FIRE OF THE FORTS.

FOR 4 DAYS NO ONE HAS BEEN ABLE TO GET BY THE FRONTIER POST!

AND WE ONLY HAVE 9 GUYS IN THIS CASEMATE!

ON 19 JUNE, IN ALSACE, THE FORTIFIED SECTOR OF THE VOSGES, AFTER AN ARTILLERY BOMBARDMENT AND ATTACK BY STUKAS, THE 215TH GERMAN DIVISION ATTACKS THE GUNSTHAL PASS. THE FRENCH BLOCKHOUSES ARE TAKEN DESPITE THE FIRE OF THE CANNONS OF FORTS FOUR À CHAUX AND HOCHWALD.

COME ON OUT!

IN LORRAINE THE GERMANS APPROACH THE SMALLER INFANTRY FORTS
THAT ARE NOT PROTECTED BY THE TURRETS OF THE LARGE FORTS.
THE 88MM AND 150MM CANNONS BLAST AWAY AT THE BLOCS AND THE
OBSERVATION POSTS. FORT BAMBESCH SURRENDERS ON 20 JUNE,
KERFENT AND HAUT POIRIER ON THE 26TH. WELSCHOFF SURRENDERS
ON THE 26TH.

NUMEROUS FORTS ARE ATTACKED. AT THE
SMALL FORTS OF EINSELING, TETING,
LAUDREFANG, MOTTENBERG, AND ROHRBACH
THE TROOPS PUT UP A GALLANT DEFENSE,
UNDER COVER OF THE ARTILLERY FIRE OF
THE LARGE FORTS.

IT'S SENSELESS TO
EXPOSE THE GARRISON
ANY LONGER.

OUR
GOVERNMENTS
ARE NEGOTIATING
AN ARMISTICE.

INTERDICTION
FIRE! AND KEEP
IT UP!

IN ALL OF THE FORTIFIED SECTORS, DESPITE THE GERMAN BOMBARDMENT, THE LARGE ARTILLERY FORTS OF BRÉHAIN,
ROCHONVILLERS, BILLIG, GALGENBERG, HACKENBERG, ANZELING AND MANY OTHERS DEFEND THE CASEMATES AND
SMALL FORTS, IN LARGE PART DUE TO THEIR CONTINUOUS, PRECISE FIRE.

SHRAPNEL SHELL,
AIM 12 TO THE
RIGHT!

IN THE FORTIFIED SECTOR OF HAGUENAU, ON 20 JUNE, AFTER A TERRIBLE BOMBARDMENT FROM CANNONS AND STUKAS,
THE 24TH GERMAN DIVISION ATTACKS THE CASEMATES OF ASCHBACH, HOFFEN, AND OBERROEDERN, COMMANDED BY THE
GRITTY LIEUTENANTS BECK, DIDIER, RIEFFEL AND VIALLE.

40.

ON THE PLATEAU OF OBERROEDERN, A LARGER FORT (PLANNED ORIGINALLY BY THE CORF) WAS REPLACED BY SEVERAL CASEMATES. FIRING WITH DETERMINATION WITH ALL THEIR GUNS, THE CREWS HELD OFF A GERMAN ATTACK THANKS ALSO TO THE CANNONS OF THE 75MM TURRETS OF FORT SCHOENENBOURG, SITUATED MORE THAN 6KM AWAY.

IN 10 DAYS, THE TWO 75MM TURRETS OF FORT SCHOENENBOURG FIRE 13,000 SHELLS. AT A NORMAL RATE OF FIRE, THE 75 CAN FIRE 80 ROUNDS IN 3 MINUTES. AGAINST A PIECE OF GROUND 40 METERS BY 30, IN AN EMERGENCY SITUATION, THE FORTRESS GUNNERS REACH A RATE OF MORE THAN 50 ROUNDS PER MINUTE. THE RANGE CAN BE 12 KILOMETERS DEPENDING ON THE MODEL OF THE CANNON.

ON 21 JUNE, AN ATTACK ON THE SMALL FORT OF FERME-CHAPPY FAILS. AFTER A VIOLENT POUNDING BY HEAVY ARTILLERY, THE GERMAN STORM TROOPS LAUNCH AN ASSAULT ON THE ENTRANCES AND THE BLOCS OF FORT FERMONT. SUPPORTED BY FORT LATIREMONT, THE DEFENSE IS EFFECTIVE. THE GERMANS PULL BACK, LEAVING THEIR DEAD AND WOUNDED BEHIND.

ON 22 JUNE, GERMAN GENERAL VON ARMIN PREPARES AN ATTACK ON FORT MOTTENBERG. THE FRENCH OBSERVERS SPOT THE PREPARATIONS FOR THE ATTACK. FORTS "MICHEL" (MICHELSBERG), HACKENBERG, ANZELING, AND MONT-DES-WELCHES HARASS THE GERMANS AND DESTROY NUMEROUS GERMAN BATTERIES. THE ATTACK IS CANCELLED.

41.

ON 17 JUNE, DURING A SPEECH ON THE RADIO, MARSHAL PÉTAIN SAYS THAT HE MUST END THE COMBAT. HE BEGINS NEGOCIATIONS FOR AN ARMISTICE. BY MEANS OF A RUSE, THE GERMANS ATTEMPT TO GET THE FORTS OF THE MAGINOT LINE TO SURRENDER, BUT EVERYWHERE THE FRENCH REFUSE TO GIVE UP.

IN THE REGION OF BITCHE, THE FORTS OF SCHIESSECK AND SIMSERHOF KEEP THE GERMANS AT A DISTANCE AND FORT ROHRBACH CONTINUES TO RESIST UP TO THE ARMISTICE. IN ALSACE, IN LORRAINE, AND IN THE ALPS, THE FORTS OF THE MAGINOT LINE FIRE MORE THAN 300,000 SHELLS AND MILLIONS OF BULLETS.

ALL COMMUNICATION IS CENTRALIZED IN THE COMMAND POST. THIS CONSISTS OF THE COMMAND POST OF THE FORT (P.C.O.), THE INFANTRY COMMAND POST, AND THE ARTILLERY COMMAND POST AS WELL AS THEIR COMMUNICATION SUPPORT SERVICES: S.R.O., S.R.I., AND S.R.A. THE INFANTRY COMMAND POST MAINTAINS THE DEFENSES OF THE FORT. THE ARTILLERY COMMAND POST DIRECTS AND MANAGES THE ARTILLERY FIRE.

FORTS FOUR À CHAUX, HOCHWALD, AND SCHOENENBOURG SUPPPORT ALL OF THE FORTS WITHIN RANGE OF THEIR CANNONS. THE LUFTWAFFE CONTINUES TO BOMBARD THE FORTS BUT IS UNABLE TO NEUTRALIZE THEM. THE FORTS PROVIDE MUTUAL SUPPORT FOR EACH OTHER. THEY FIRE ABOVE THEIR NEIGHBORS IN ORDER TO INTERFERE WITH THE ACCURACY OF THE STUKAS.

42

TWO STUKA SQUADRONS BOMBARD FORT SCHOENENBOURG 6 TIMES. TWO GIANT 305 AND 420MM MORTARS FIRE AT THE FORT OVER A 3 DAY PERIOD. SCHOENENBOURG IS HIT BY MORE THAN 3000 BOMBS AND SHELLS. THIS GIVES SCHOENENBOURG THE UNFORTUNATE RECORD OF BEING THE MOST BOMBED FORT OF ALL THE MAGINOT LINE.

NEGOTIATIONS WITH GERMANY AND ITALY ARE COMPLETED. THE GUNS ARE SILENT. THE ARMISTICE GOES INTO EFFECT ON TUESDAY, 25 JUNE 1940 AT 0035 HOURS. IN ALSACE-LORRAINE AND IN THE ALPS, 90% OF THE FORTS OF THE MAGINOT LINE CONTINUE TO RESIST. ALL OF THEIR WEAPONS ARE OPERATIONAL.

ON JUNE 25, 1940, THE FRENCH ARMY HIGH COMMAND WAS UNAWARE THAT, IN ALSACE AND LORRAINE, THE FORTS OF THE MAGINOT LINE CONTINUED TO RESIST. THREATENED BY HITLER, GENERAL HUNTZIGER, THE CHIEF FRENCH DELEGATE OF THE ARMISTICE COMMISSION MEETING AT WIESBADEN, GERMANY, SENT 3 FRENCH COLONELS TO THE FORTIFIED SECTORS.

GOOD DAY, COLONEL. HAVE YOU COME WITH TRUCKS TO TAKE US TO THE FREE ZONE?

I'M SO SORRY. DESPITE YOUR MAGNIFICENT RESISTANCE, YOU ARE NOW CONSIDERED PRISONERS OF WAR!

IN ALSACE-LORRAINE, THE UNDEFEATED GARRISONS ARE LITERALLY DELIVERED TO THE GERMANS. THE FORTS AND THE ARMAMENTS MUST BE HANDED OVER TO THE WEHRMACHT IN GOOD CONDITION. CONTRARY TO ORDERS RECEIVED, THE FRENCH DESTROY ALL OF THEIR DOCUMENTS, TOPOGRAPHIC MAPS AND FIRING CHARTS.

BUT MOST OF FRANCE IS OCCUPIED!

WE FOUGHT WELL!

IT'S TAKEN US 2 YEARS TO PUT TOGETHER THESE OBSERVATION AND FIRING CHARTS!

BETTER TO BURN IT SO THE GERMANS CAN'T USE IT!

IN THE ALPS, AFTER THE ARMISTICE, THE FRENCH EVACUATE THE ADVANCE POSTS AND THE FORTS. THEY ARE ABANDONED AND WILL BE DEMOBILIZED, PART OF THE NON-OCCUPIED ZONE.

OFFICIAL MESSAGE WRITTEN BY THE COMMANDER-IN-CHIEF OF THE FRENCH ARMY, ADDRESSED TO ALL THE GARRISONS OF THE MAGINOT LINE.

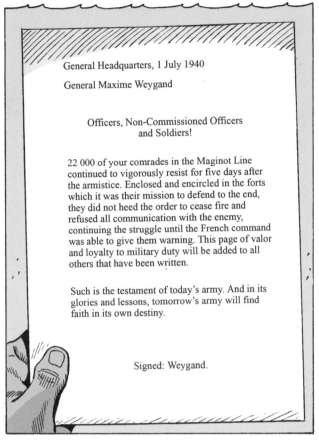

General Headquarters, 1 July 1940

General Maxime Weygand

Officers, Non-Commissioned Officers and Soldiers!

22 000 of your comrades in the Maginot Line continued to vigorously resist for five days after the armistice. Enclosed and encircled in the forts which it was their mission to defend to the end, they did not heed the order to cease fire and refused all communication with the enemy, continuing the struggle until the French command was able to give them warning. This page of valor and loyalty to military duty will be added to all others that have been written.

Such is the testament of today's army. And in its glories and lessons, tomorrow's army will find faith in its own destiny.

Signed: Weygand.

IN THE NORTHEAST THE GERMAN OFFICERS NOTIFY THE FRENCH SOLDIERS THAT THEY ARE PRISONERS OF WAR. FROM 27 JUNE TO 2 JULY THE TROOPS LEAVE THEIR CONCRETE PROTECTION AND HEAD TOWARDS THE UNKNOWN.

THE VALIANT DEFENDERS OF THE MAGINOT LINE LEAVE ON FOOT FOR THE P.O.W. CAMPS IN FRANCE. BY THE END OF AUGUST 1940 THEY WILL BE SENT TO STALAGS IN GERMANY WHERE THEY WILL REMAIN FOR THE NEXT 5 YEARS.

FROM JULY 1940 THE GERMANS TOOK POSSESSION OF THE FORTIFICATIONS. OVER THE NEXT FEW WEEKS, SMALL CREWS OF ENGINEERS STAY IN THE FORTS TO EXPLAIN TO THE NEW OCCUPANTS HOW EVERYTHING WORKS.

AT THE END OF THE MONTH OF JULY 1940, NAZI PROPAGANDA FILM CREWS ARRIVE FROM BERLIN. THE GERMANS RE-ENACT ON FILM THE ATTACK ON THE MAGINOT LINE. MANY SEQUENCES ARE FILMED AT SCHOENENBOURG. TO THE PRESENT TIME THE FILM "SIEG IM WESTEN" (VICTORY IN THE WEST) IS STILL USED AS A DOCUMENTARY.

IN 1941, THE GERMAN ENGINEERS OF THE WEHRMACHT EXPERIMENT WITH NEW EXPLOSIVE TECHNIQUES ON THE CONCRETE AND ARMOR OF THE FORTS. BILLIG, FOUR À CHAUX AND MÉTRICH ARE SERIOUSLY DAMAGED.

THE GERMANS TEAR UP THE ANTI-TANK RAILS TO SALVAGE THE METAL. THEY DISASSEMBLE MUCH OF THE MATERIAL IN THE FORTS; ALL OF IT IS USED IN THE SUBMARINE BASES THE NAZIS BUILT ALONG THE ATLANTIC COAST.

THE NAZIS TRANSFORM THE MUNITIONS STORAGE MAGAZINES AND UNDERGROUND TUNNELS INTO FACTORIES. FORTS HACKENBERG, HOCHWALD, MÉTRICH, AND MICHELSBERG ARE USED TO BUILD AIRCRAFT MOTORS OR RIFLE PARTS. OTHER FORTS LIKE SIMSERHOF AND MOLVANGE SERVE AS MATERIAL STORAGE DEPOTS.

1943: IN TUNISIA, THE AFRIKA KORPS AND ITALIAN TROOPS USE THE CASEMATES OF THE FORMER FRENCH MARETH LINE TO HOLD OFF FOR ONE MONTH AN ATTACK BY THE BRITISH EIGHTH ARMY WHO HAS COME TO LIBERATE NORTH AFRICA.

IN NOVEMBER 1944 THE AMERICAN ARMY CROSSES THE MOSELLE RIVER. THE GERMANS HUNKER DOWN INSIDE FORT HACKENBERG AND FIRE ON THE 90TH INFANTRY DIVISION. BLOC 8 IS NEUTRALIZED BY THE AMERICAN HEAVY ARTILLERY AND TANKS. IN DECEMBER, THE WEHRMACHT HOLDS OUT IN FORTS SIMSERHOF AND SCHIESSECK. THE 44TH AND 100TH INFANTRY DIVISIONS, SUPPORTED BY THE AIR FORCE AND THE ENGINEERS, TAKE SEVEN DAYS TO CAPTURE THE FORTS.

46.

IN THE FALL OF 1944, IN THE ALPS, THE FRENCH ENGAGE IN DIFFICULT COMBAT WITH THE GERMAN MOUNTAINEERS AND ITALIAN ALPINI TROOPS. FORT SAPEY IS CAPTURED BY FRENCH ALPINE TROOPS. IN THE BEGINNING OF 1945 THE AMERICANS OCCUPY MONTE-GROSSO. IN APRIL THE ALLIES ATTACK THE FORTS OF THE AUTHION SECTOR, AND THE FRENCH RECAPTURE FORTS ROCHE-LA-CROIX AND PLAN CAVAL. FIGHTING DOESN'T STOP UNTIL THE ARMISTICE OF 8 MAY 1945.

THE GERMANS DESTROY A NUMBER OF FORTS PRIOR TO THEIR PULL OUT. IN EUROPE, THE WAR IS FINISHED ON 8 MAY 1945. IN 1946, GENERAL FORTIN OF THE FRENCH ENGINEERS TAKES AN INVENTORY OF THE FORTIFIED LINE IN THE NORTHEAST. WITH A LIMITED BUDGET HE HIRES 200 CIVIL ENGINEERS TO PROCEED WITH IMMEDIATE REPAIRS.

NOT EASY TO FIGHT AT 2000M IN MINUS 20-DEGREE WEATHER!

I THINK THEY'VE FORGOTTEN ABOUT US UP HERE. WE DON'T HAVE THE BEST EQUIPMENT!

WHEN THE GERMANS PULLED OUT AT THE END OF '44, THEY DID AS MUCH DAMAGE AS POSSIBLE!

OUR INVENTORY SHOWS THAT NOT MORE THAN 10% OF THE WEAPONS ARE STILL IN PLACE!

FACING SUPERIOR FORCES OF THE SOVIET UNION, IT IS BELIEVED THAT THE FORTIFICATIONS COULD PLAY A SIGNIFICANT ROLE IN THE DEFENSE OF FRANCE. IN 1950 THE TECHNICAL FORTIFICATIONS COMMITTEE (C.T.F.) IS CREATED. IT IS LED BY GENERAL LAFFARGE, THEN DOMARD. REPAIR WORK BEGINS.

THIS MUST BE ABLE TO WITHSTAND AN ATOMIC BOMB!

THAT'S WHY WE'VE MODIFIED THE VENTILATION SYSTEM TO SUCK THE AIR THROUGH THE ROCK!

THE NEW CUPOLAS ARE WELL INTEGRATED INTO THE BLOC, MAKING THEM MUCH LESS VULNERABLE.

THE TURRETS WERE REMOVED AND REBUILT.

ON 8 JANUARY 1951, A BUDGET IS PASSED AUTHORIZING 2 BILLION FRANCS (46 MILLION EUROS= 65 MILLION DOLLARS). ONLY THE LARGEST FORTS OF THE NORTHEAST ARE REPAIRED. NEW TESTS ARE CONDUCTED ON MODERN WEAPON PROTOTYPES. FOUR À CHAUX RECEIVES A NEW 81MM TURRET. THE MEN'S ENTRANCE OF SCHOENENBOURG IS COMPLETELY MODIFIED.

47.

BEGINNING IN 1957, FORT HOCHWALD IS TRANSFORMED. IT BECOMES THE MOST POWERFUL RADAR STATION IN EUROPE TO KEEP WATCH ON WARSAW PACT FORCES. IN THE SOUTH THE RADAR STATION OF MONT AGEL SURVEYS THE MEDITERRANEAN. THE U.S. AIR FORCE MAKES USE, ON OCCASION, OF FORT MOLVANGE AND TETING, BUT THE MAGINOT LINE DOES NOT INTEREST NATO.

1960: THE EXPLOSION OF THE FIRST FRENCH ATOM BOMB. THE MAGINOT LINE WILL NO LONGER PLAY A ROLE IN THE DEFENSE OF FRANCE. IN 1966 FRANCE LEAVES NATO. THE UPKEEP OF THE LARGE FORTS ENDS IN 1967. BEGINNING IN 1968 THE STATE PUTS SOME CASEMATES AND SMALL FORTS UP FOR SALE. FORT ROCHONVILLERS IS USED AS A COMMAND POST FOR THE 1ST FRENCH ARMY FROM 1981 TO 1998.

THE SMALL FORTS ARE SOLD TO THE LOCAL COMMUNITIES OR TO INDIVIDUALS. SOME ARE USED AS VACATION HOMES OR MUSHROOM FARMS. SALVAGERS COME IN TO RECUPERATE THE METAL. VANDALS PILLAGE THE UNDERGROUND. IN 1997 THE ARMY BURIES CERTAIN ENTRANCES TO KEEP INTRUDERS OUT. SINCE 1999 THE ARMY HAS AUTHORIZED THE ASSOCIATIONS TO REMOVE AND SAFEGUARD MATERIALS LEFT IN THE FORTS.

IN FRANCE, AFTER THE WAR, THE MAGINOT LINE HAS BECOME A SCAPEGOAT, RESPONSIBLE FOR THE DEFEAT OF 1940. VETERANS BEGIN A LONG STRUGGLE TO REHABILITATE ITS REPUTATION. THE FRENCH FORTIFICATIONS HAVE PLAYED THE EXACT ROLE FOR WHICH THEY WERE PLANNED. SINCE 1977, A NUMBER OF ASSOCIATIONS HAVE PASSIONATELY RESTORED CERTAIN FORTS AND OPENED THEM FOR VISITS. EACH YEAR, CLOSE TO 300,000 TOURISTS COME TO DISCOVER THE MAGINOT LINE...

NOVEMBER 2009
MARC HALTER

48.

Translation by
Randa DUVICK & Clayton DONNELL

Randa DUVICK, Professor of French
Chair, Department of Foreign Langages & Literatures
Valparaison University IN, USA

Clayton DONNELL, An American who has a degree in history
and has passionately studied European military history for
30 years. He is co-author of "Modern European Military
Fortifications" – PRAEGER, 2004.
He created an internet website in English on the Maginot Line
and has written 3 books about fortifications for OSPREY.

First edition in English

PUBLICATION AND RIGHTS RESERVED
Association Moselle River 1944® – F 57940
www.moselleriver.org

PRODUCTION and TECHNICAL COORDINATION
Marc Halter,
Pascal Moretti
Jean Pascal Speck

INFORMATION
E.mail: info@moselleriver.org

ORDER
www.moselleriver.org

ISBN : 978-2-9523092-5-7
Dépot légal : 07-2011

Achevé d'imprimer juin 2011
sur les presses de l'Imprimerie L'Huillier
(F - 57190) Florange